HTA + VBSCRIPT

+

MICROSOFT.JET.O LEDB.3.51 = YOU CODE SMARTER AND FASTER

Please Judge this book by its cover.
The program is inside

Richard Edwards

STOP WISHING FOR IT

It is right here

Looking for something you or a friend of yours could use to charge up your new year with a program that works to produce results. Here it is!

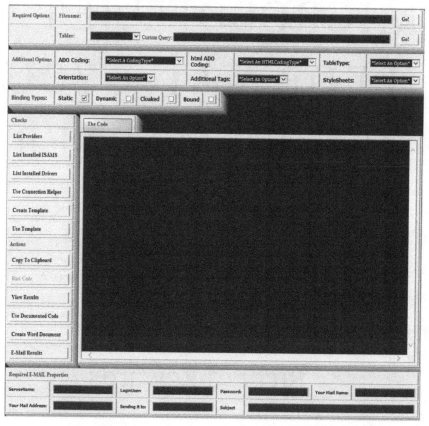

This one uses Microsoft.Jet.OleDb.3.51 and the code to make it is in this book. So, what does it do?

Well, for one thing you can open all older versions of Access databases with the extension of .mdb. But they had to be created between 1998 and 2007. Otherwise, you will get an error telling you that the database was created by a newer version of Access.

Purchase the version of this product – past that time – that is in sync with the provider requirements. I have one for each version of the ACE.OLEDB provider up to Microsoft.ACE.OLEDB.15.0.

When you click the first Go button at the very top and right of the program, brings up a common dialog box:

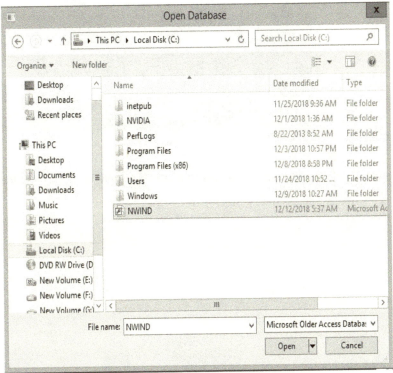

Which I used to connect to an older database file: NWind.mdb.

Once I have done this, I click the other go button which lists all the tables and views and automates the process of creating creatable queries as seen below:

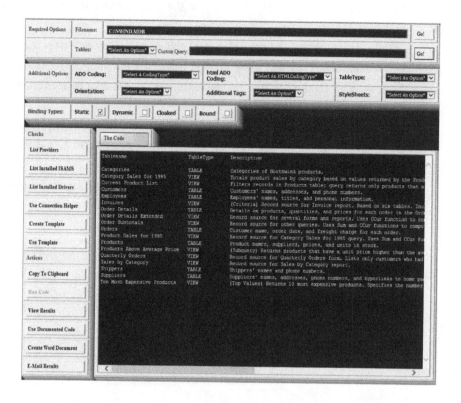

Once I decide which Query to run, because the table type, orientation and control type are set to table, Multi-Line Horizontal and span, respectively html code is generated:

```
<html>
<head>
<title>Products</title>
<style type='text/css'>
body
{
    PADDING-RIGHT: 0px;
    PADDING-LEFT: 0px;
    PADDING-BOTTOM: 0px;
    MARGIN: 0px;
    COLOR: #333;
    PADDING-TOP: 0px;
    FONT-FAMILY: verdana, arial, helvetica, sans-serif;
}
table
{
    BORDER-RIGHT: #999999 3px solid;
    PADDING-RIGHT: 6px;
    PADDING-LEFT: 6px;
    FONT-WEIGHT: Bold;
    FONT-SIZE: 14px;
    PADDING-BOTTOM: 6px;
    COLOR: Peru;
    LINE-HEIGHT: 14px;
    PADDING-TOP: 6px;
    BORDER-BOTTOM: #999 1px solid;
    BACKGROUND-COLOR: #eeeeee;
    FONT-FAMILY: verdana, arial, helvetica, sans-serif;
    FONT-SIZE: 12px;
}
th
{
```

This is what the code looks like inside the program. Of course, it is a lot clearer in the program than the image shows. At this point, clicking on View Results on the left side of the screen:

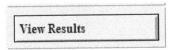
View Results

Will show you this:

ProductID	ProductName	SupplierID	CategoryID	QuantityPerUnit
1	Chai	1	1	10 boxes x 20 bags
2	Chang	1	1	24 - 12 oz bottles
3	Aniseed Syrup	1	2	12 - 550 ml bottles
4	Chef Anton	2	2	48 - 6 oz jars
5	Chef Anton	2	2	36 boxes
6	Grandma	3	2	12 - 8 oz jars
7	Uncle Bob	3	7	12 - 1 lb pkgs.
8	Northwoods Cranberry Sauce	3	2	12 - 12 oz jars
9	Mishi Kobe Niku	4	6	18 - 500 g pkgs.
10	Ikura	4	8	12 - 200 ml jars
11	Queso Cabrales	5	4	1 kg pkg.
12	Queso Manchego La Pastora	5	4	10 - 500 g pkgs.

Of course, how flashy it looks will depend on the stylesheet that you use and the additional tag that you partnered with it.

What is being offered

There is no such thing as a bugless program. Glitches happen. However, the routines – for static, dynamic, cloaked and bound have been tested and work. Additionally, the HTML ADO Coding option, pictured below, only works with the Bound coding option.

You have four basic formats:

Binding Types:	Static	☑	Dynamic	☐	Cloaked	☐	Bound	☐

Each one of these formats allows you to mix Table types: Report or table; Orientation: Multi-Line Horizontal, Multi-Line Vertical, Single-Line Horizontal and Single Line vertical; Additional Tags: Button, Combobox, Div, Listbox, Span, Textarea and Textbox; and 10 style sheets.

Meaning you have 560 ways to create Static, Dynamic, Cloaked or Bound outputs and that there are 2,240 ways you can produce html code from one database and one table.

If each only averaged 30 lines of code, those 2.240 ways to produce code would be the same outcome as one programmer could create in a year. The Products table using the Shadow Box stylesheet, came out to 1,114 lines and that took about 30 seconds to produce and display. And that is from the time the program started up to the time the view the results button was clicked on.

This program can list all the providers, drivers and ISAMS that are installed on the machine the program is running on, too.

The e-mail program is designed to be used with your Gmail account. If you don't have one, well, its probably not something you'd get any warm and fuzzies from.

If you do, the newer version of Gmail, has a switch that must be enabled in order to use it.

THE CODE NEEDED TO MAKE THIS PROGRAM WORK FOR YOU

From below the line is the code you need to create this program:

```
<html xmlns:v="urn:schemas-microsoft-com:vml">
<HEAD>
<HTA:Application
    ID = "Excalibur"
    APPLICATIONNAME = "Excalibur"
    Scroll = "no"
    SINGLEINSTANCE = "No"
    WORKSTATE = "Normal"
>
<head>
<title>Excalibur</title>
<style type='text/css'>
v\:*{ behavior: url(#default#VML);}
body
{
    PADDING-RIGHT: 0px;
    PADDING-LEFT: 0px;
    PADDING-BOTTOM: 0px;
    MARGIN: 0px;
    COLOR: #333;
```

```
    PADDING-TOP: 0px;
    FONT-FAMILY: verdana, arial, helvetica, sans-serif;
}
Table
{
    BORDER-RIGHT: #999999 1px solid;
    PADDING-RIGHT: 1px;
    PADDING-LEFT: 1px;
    PADDING-BOTTOM: 1px;
    LINE-HEIGHT: 8px;
    PADDING-TOP: 1px;
    BORDER-BOTTOM: #999 1px solid;
    BACKGROUND-COLOR: #eeeeee;
    filter:progid:DXImageTransform.Microsoft.Shadow(color='silver',
Direction=135, Strength=16)
}
th
{
    BORDER-RIGHT: #999999 3px solid;
    PADDING-RIGHT: 6px;
    PADDING-LEFT: 6px;
    FONT-WEIGHT: Bold;
    FONT-SIZE: 14px;
    PADDING-BOTTOM: 6px;
    COLOR: darkred;
    LINE-HEIGHT: 14px;
    PADDING-TOP: 6px;
    BORDER-BOTTOM: #999 1px solid;
    BACKGROUND-COLOR: #eeeeee;
    FONT-FAMILY: font-family: Cambria, serif;
    FONT-SIZE: 12px;
    text-align: left;
    white-Space: nowrap;
}
.th
{
    BORDER-RIGHT: #999999 2px solid;
    PADDING-RIGHT: 6px;
    PADDING-LEFT: 6px;
    FONT-WEIGHT: Bold;
```

```
    PADDING-BOTTOM: 6px;
    COLOR: black;
    PADDING-TOP: 6px;
    BORDER-BOTTOM: #999 2px solid;
    BACKGROUND-COLOR: #eeeeee;
    FONT-FAMILY: font-family: Cambria, serif;
    FONT-SIZE: 10px;
    text-align: right;
    white-Space: nowrap;
}
td
{
    BORDER-RIGHT: #999999 3px solid;
    PADDING-RIGHT: 6px;
    PADDING-LEFT: 6px;
    FONT-WEIGHT: Normal;
    PADDING-BOTTOM: 6px;
    COLOR: navy;
    LINE-HEIGHT: 14px;
    PADDING-TOP: 6px;
    BORDER-BOTTOM: #999 1px solid;
    BACKGROUND-COLOR: #eeeeee;
    FONT-FAMILY: font-family: Cambria, serif;
    FONT-SIZE: 12px;
    text-align: left;
    white-Space: nowrap;
}
div
{
    BORDER-RIGHT: #999999 3px solid;
    PADDING-RIGHT: 6px;
    PADDING-LEFT: 6px;
    FONT-WEIGHT: Normal;
    PADDING-BOTTOM: 6px;
    COLOR: white;
    PADDING-TOP: 6px;
    BORDER-BOTTOM: #999 1px solid;
    BACKGROUND-COLOR: navy;
    FONT-FAMILY: font-family: Cambria, serif;
    FONT-SIZE: 10px;
```

```css
    text-align: left;
    white-Space: nowrap;
}
span
{
    BORDER-RIGHT: #999999 3px solid;
    PADDING-RIGHT: 3px;
    PADDING-LEFT: 3px;
    FONT-WEIGHT: Normal;
    PADDING-BOTTOM: 3px;
    COLOR: white;
    PADDING-TOP: 3px;
    BORDER-BOTTOM: #999 1px solid;
    BACKGROUND-COLOR: navy;
    FONT-FAMILY: font-family: Cambria, serif;
    FONT-SIZE: 10px;
    text-align: left;
    white-Space: nowrap;
    display: inline-block;
    width: 100%;
}
textarea
{
    BORDER-RIGHT: #999999 3px solid;
    PADDING-RIGHT: 3px;
    PADDING-LEFT: 3px;
    FONT-WEIGHT: Normal;
    PADDING-BOTTOM: 3px;
    COLOR: white;
    PADDING-TOP: 3px;
    BORDER-BOTTOM: #999 1px solid;
    BACKGROUND-COLOR: navy;
    FONT-FAMILY: font-family: Cambria, serif;
    FONT-SIZE: 12px;
    text-align: left;
    width: 100%;
}
select
{
    BORDER-RIGHT: #999999 1px solid;
```

```
    PADDING-RIGHT: 1px;
    PADDING-LEFT: 1px;
    FONT-WEIGHT: Normal;
    PADDING-BOTTOM: 1px;
    COLOR: white;
    PADDING-TOP: 1px;
    BORDER-BOTTOM: #999 1px solid;
    BACKGROUND-COLOR: navy;
    FONT-FAMILY: Cambria, serif;
    FONT-SIZE: 12px;
    text-align: left;
    white-Space: nowrap;
    width: 450px;
}
select1
{
    BORDER-RIGHT: #999999 1px solid;
    PADDING-RIGHT: 1px;
    PADDING-LEFT: 1px;
    FONT-WEIGHT: Normal;
    PADDING-BOTTOM: 1px;
    COLOR: white;
    PADDING-TOP: 1px;
    BORDER-BOTTOM: #999 1px solid;
    BACKGROUND-COLOR: navy;
    FONT-FAMILY: Cambria, serif;
    FONT-SIZE: 12px;
    text-align: left;
    white-Space: nowrap;
    width: 450px;
}
select2
{
    BORDER-RIGHT: #999999 1px solid;
    PADDING-RIGHT: 1px;
    PADDING-LEFT: 1px;
    FONT-WEIGHT: Normal;
    PADDING-BOTTOM: 1px;
    COLOR: white;
    PADDING-TOP: 1px;
```

```css
    BORDER-BOTTOM: #999 1px solid;
    BACKGROUND-COLOR: navy;
    FONT-FAMILY: Cambria, serif;
    FONT-SIZE: 12px;
    text-align: left;
    white-Space: nowrap;
    width: 450px;
}
#select
{
    BORDER-RIGHT: #999999 1px solid;
    PADDING-RIGHT: 1px;
    PADDING-LEFT: 1px;
    FONT-WEIGHT: Normal;
    PADDING-BOTTOM: 1px;
    COLOR: white;
    PADDING-TOP: 1px;
    BORDER-BOTTOM: #999 1px solid;
    BACKGROUND-COLOR: navy;
    FONT-FAMILY: Cambria, serif;
    FONT-SIZE: 12px;
    text-align: left;
    white-Space: nowrap;
    width: 100px;
}
select4
{
    BORDER-RIGHT: #999999 1px solid;
    PADDING-RIGHT: 1px;
    PADDING-LEFT: 1px;
    FONT-WEIGHT: Normal;
    PADDING-BOTTOM: 1px;
    COLOR: white;
    PADDING-TOP: 1px;
    BORDER-BOTTOM: #999 1px solid;
    BACKGROUND-COLOR: navy;
    FONT-FAMILY: Cambria, serif;
    FONT-SIZE: 12px;
    text-align: left;
    white-Space: nowrap;
```

```
        width: 254px;
    }
    input
    {
        BORDER-RIGHT: #999999 3px solid;
        PADDING-RIGHT: 3px;
        PADDING-LEFT: 3px;
        FONT-WEIGHT: Bold;
        PADDING-BOTTOM: 3px;
        COLOR: white;
        PADDING-TOP: 3px;
        BORDER-BOTTOM: #999 1px solid;
        BACKGROUND-COLOR: navy;
        FONT-FAMILY: font-family: Cambria, serif;
        FONT-SIZE: 12px;
        text-align: left;
        display: table-cell;
        white-Space: nowrap;
        width: 100%;
    }
    </style>
    <body BGColor=#242424>
    <table            style="Position:Absolute;Top:0px;Left:0px;Width:900px;Font-
family:Tahoma;font-size:10px">
    <tr><th  class=tdbackground  align=Right  Width=100px  nowrap>Required
Options</th>
    <th align=right style="Width:77px;" nowrap><b>Filename:</b></th>
    <td  align=left  nowrap><input  Type='text'  id='FName'  name='FName'
style='width:750px;'></input></td>
    <td><input         Type='Button'         id='Search'         name='Search'
style='width:50px;Background-color:ButtonFace;color:black;'
Value="Go!"></input></td>
    </tr>
    <tr>
    <tr><th class=tdbackground align=Right Width=115px nowrap> </th>
    <th align=right Width=77px nowrap><b>Tables: </b></th>
    <td   align=left   nowrap><select   id="trex"   style="width:125px;background-
Color:navy;Color:White;"                    onChange="HandlestrexChange()"
name="trexPullDown"></select>
```

```
Custom    Query: <input    Type='text'    id='CQuery'    name=CQuery'
style='width:540px;'></input>
    </td>
    <td><input Type='Button' id='LT1' name='LT1' style='width:50px;Background-
color:ButtonFace;color:black;' Value="Go!"></input></td></tr>
    </table>


    <table            style="Position:Absolute;Top:100px;Left:0px;Width:900px;Font-
family:Tahoma;font-size:10px">
    <tr><th class=tdbackground align=Center nowrap>Additional Options</th>
    <th        class="myclass"        Style="color:Black;font-family:Tahoma;font-
size:12px;width:115px;" Align=Right Nowrap>ADO Coding:</TH>
    <th><SELECT              ID="ADOCoding"              class="myclass1"
style="width:195px;background-Color:navy;Color:White"
onChange="HandlesEngineTypeChange()" name="EngineTypePullDown">
    <option Value="*Select A CodingType*">*Select A CodingType*</option>
    <option Value="cncmdrs">Connection Command And Recordset</option>
    <option Value="cnrs">Connection And Recordset</option>
    <option Value="cmdrs">Command And Recordset</option>
    <option Value="rs">Recordset</option>
    </SELECT></th>
    <th        class="myclass"        Style="color:Black;font-family:Tahoma;font-
size:12px;width:115px;" Align=Right Nowrap>html ADO Coding:</TH>
    <th><SELECT              ID="HTMLADOCoding"              class="myclass1"
style="width:195px;background-Color:navy;Color:White"
onChange="HandlesHTMLEngineTypeChange()"
name="HTMLEngineTypePullDown">
    <option    Value="*Select    An    HTMLCodingType*">*Select    An
HTMLCodingType*</option>
    <option Value="cncmdrs">Connection Command And Recordset</option>
    <option Value="cnrs">Connection And Recordset</option>
    <option Value="cmdrs">Command And Recordset</option>
    <option Value="rs">Recordset</option>
    </SELECT></th>
    <th        class="myclass"        Style="color:Black;font-family:Tahoma;font-
size:12px;width:115px;" Align=Right Nowrap>TableType:</TH>
    <th><SELECT              ID="TableType"              class="myclass1"
style="width:125px;background-Color:navy;Color:White"
onChange="HandlesTableTypeChange()" name="TableTypePullDown">
    <option Value="*Select A TableType*">*Select An Option*</option>
```

```html
<option Value="Table">Table</option>
<option Value="Report">Report</option>
</SELECT></th>
</tr>
<tr>
<th class=tdbackground align=Center nowrap> </th><th class="myclass"
Style="color:Black;font-family:Tahoma;font-size:12px"    Align=Right    nowrap>
Orientation:</TH>
<th>
<SELECT            class="myclass1"              style="width:125px;background-
Color:navy;Color:White"            onChange="HandlesOrientationChange()"
name="OrientationPullDown">
<option selected Value="*Select An Orientation*">*Select An Option*</option>
<option Value="Multi-Line Horizontal">Multi-Line Horizontal</option>
<option Value="Multi-Line Vertical">Multi-Line Vertical</option>
<option Value="Single-Line Horizontal">Single-Line Horizontal</option>
<option Value="Single-Line Vertical">Single-Line Vertical</option>
</SELECT></TH>
<TH   class="myclass"   Style="color:Black;font-family:Tahoma;font-size:12px"
Align=Right nowrap>    Additional Tags:</TH>
<TH>
<SELECT            class="myclass1"              style="width:125px;background-
Color:navy;Color:White"            onChange="HandlesControlTypeChange()"
name="ControlTypePullDown">
<option   selected   Value="*Select   An   Additional   Tag*">*Select   An
Option*</option>
<option Value="Button">Button</option>
<option Value="Combobox">Combobox</option>
<option Value="Div">Div</option>
<option Value="Listbox">Listbox</option>
<option Value="Span">Span</option>
<option Value="Textarea">Textarea</option>
<option Value="Textbox">Textbox</option>
</SELECT></TH>
<TH   class="myclass"   Style="color:Black;font-family:Tahoma;font-size:12px"
Align=Right nowrap>    StyleSheets:</TH>
<TH>
<SELECT            class="myclass"              style="width:125px;background-
Color:navy;Color:White"            onChange="HandlesStyleSheetChange()"
name="StyleSheetPullDown">
```

```html
<option selected Value="*Select A StyleSheet*">*Select An Option*</option>
<option Value="None">None</option>
<option Value="Basic">Basic</option>
<option Value="InLine">InLine</option>
<option Value="BlackAndWhiteText">Black And White Text</option>
<option Value="OscillatingRowColors">Oscillating Row Colors</option>
<option Value="ColoredText">Colored Text</option>
<option Value="GhostDecorated">Ghost Decorated</Option>
<option Value="3D">3d</option>
<option Value="ShadowBox">Shadow Box</option>
<option Value="Customized">Customized</options>
</select></TH></TR>
</table>
<table          style="Position:Absolute;Top:190px;Left:0px;Width:400px;Font-
family:Tahoma;font-size:10px">
  <tr><th          class="myclass"          Style="background-
Color:buttonface;color:darkred;font-family:Tahoma;font-size:12px;Width:115px"
Align=Right nowrap>Binding Types:</th>
  <th Style="background-Color:buttonface;color:Black;font-family:Tahoma;font-
size:12px" Align=Right nowrap>Static</th>
  <th><input     type='checkbox'     id='st'     name='st'     checked=true
style="width:25px;background-Color:buttonface;Color:black"></input></th>
  <th Style="background-Color:buttonface;color:Black;font-family:Tahoma;font-
size:12px" Align=Right nowrap>Dynamic</th>
  <th><input     type='checkbox'     id='dynamic'     name='dynamic'
style="width:25px;background-Color:buttonface;Color:black"></input></th>
  <th Style="background-Color:buttonface;color:Black;font-family:Tahoma;font-
size:12px" Align=Right nowrap>Cloaked</th>
  <th><input     type='checkbox'     id='cloaked'     name='cloaked'
style="width:25px;background-Color:buttonface;Color:black"></input></th>
  <th Style="background-Color:buttonface;color:Black;font-family:Tahoma;font-
size:12px" Align=Right nowrap>Bound</th>
  <th><input     type='checkbox'     id='bound'     name='bound'
style="width:25px;background-Color:buttonface;Color:black"></input></th>
  </tr>
</table>
<table   style="Position:Absolute;Top:245px;Left:0px;Font-family:Tahoma;font-
size:10px">
  <TR><TH   class=td   background   align=Center   nowrap
colspan=6>Checks</TH></TR>
```

```
<TR>
<TH align=left nowrap>
<input          Type='Button'          id='Providers'          name='Providers'
style='width:150px;Background-color:ButtonFace;color:black;'          Value="List
Providers"></input>
</TH></TR>
<TR>
<TH align=left nowrap>
<input          Type='Button'          id='ISAMS'          name='ISAMS'
style='width:150px;Background-color:ButtonFace;color:black;' Value="List Installed
ISAMS"></input>
</TH></TR>
<TR>
<TH align=left nowrap">
<input          Type='Button'          id='Drivers'          name='Drivers'
style='width:150px;Background-color:ButtonFace;color:black;' Value="List Installed
Drivers"></input>
</th></tr>
<TR>
<TH align=left nowrap>
<input          Type='Button'          id='DataLinks1'          name='DataLinks1'
style='width:150px;Background-color:ButtonFace;color:black;'          Value="Use
Connection Helper"></input>
</TH></TR>
<TR>
<TH align=left nowrap">
<input      Type='Button'      id='Createtemplate'      name='CreateTemplate'
style='width:150px;Background-color:ButtonFace;color:black;'          Value="Create
Template"></input>
</TH></TR>
<TH align=left nowrap>
<input          Type='Button'          id='UseTemplate'          name='UseTemplate'
style='width:150px;Background-color:ButtonFace;color:black;'          Value="Use
Template"></input>
</TH></TR>
<TR><TH          class=td          background          align=Center          nowrap
colspan=5>Actions</TH></TR>
<TR>
<TH align=left nowrap>
```

```html
    <input          Type='Button'          id='Clipboard1'          name='Clipboard1'
style='width:150px;Background-color:ButtonFace;color:black;'    Value="Copy    To
Clipboard"></input>
    </TH>
    </TR>
    <TR>
    <TH align=left nowrap>
    <input          Type='Button'          id='RunMe'          name='RunMe'
style='width:150px;Background-color:ButtonFace;color:black;'          Value="Run
Code"></input>
    </TH></TR>
    <TR>
    <TH align=left nowrap>
    <input          Type='Button'          id='ViewMe'          name='ViewMe'
style='width:150px;Background-color:ButtonFace;color:black;'          Value="View
Results"></input>
    </TH></TR>
    <TR>
    <TH align=left nowrap>
    <input          Type='Button'          id='Document'          name='Documenter'
style='width:150px;Background-color:ButtonFace;color:black;'          Value="Use
Documented Code"></input>
    </TH></TR>

    <TR><TH    align=left    nowrap><input    Type='Button'    id='wd'    name='wd'
style='width:150px;Background-color:ButtonFace;color:black;'    Value="Create    Word
Document"></input></TH></TR>

    <TR>
    <TH align=left nowrap>
    <input          Type='Button'          id='EMAIL'          name='EMAIL'
style='width:150px;Background-color:ButtonFace;color:black;'          Value="E-Mail
Results"></input>
    </TH></TR>
    </table>
    </table>

    <TABLE                    style="Position:Absolute;Top:245px;Left:180px;Font-
family:Tahoma;font-size:10px">
    <TR><TH>
```

```html
<v:roundrect id="A" style="width:120;height:30px" arcsize="5%">
<v:fill color="#CCCCCC" color2="white" Opacity=90% Opacity2=90%
method="linear sigma" angle="-135" type="gradientradial" />
<v:textbox id="A1" style="font-family:Garmond;Font-
size:12px;Color:darkred"><b>The Code</b></v:textbox>
<v:shadow id="A2" on="false" offset="3pt, 3pt" opacity="70%"
color="black"/>
</v:roundrect>
</TH></TR>
</TABLE>
<TABLE style="border:solid;border-color:Blue;border-
width:1px;Position:Absolute;Left:180;Top:285px;width:832px;Height:505px">
<TR><TH><Textarea ID="Textarea1" name="Textarea1" Style="font-
family:Courier New;Height:505px;Width:832px;"
wrap="off"></textarea></TH></TR>
</TABLE>


<Table class="myclass" Style="border:outset;border-color:Silver;border-
width:1px;position:absolute;top:820px;left:0px;">
<tr><th class=tdbackground align=Center nowrap colspan=10>Required E-MAIL
Properties</th></tr>
<TR><TH class="myclass" Style="color:Black;font-family:Tahoma;font-
size:10px" Align=Right Nowrap>ServerName:</TH>
<th>
<Input type='text' id=sn style="width:150px;background-
Color:navy;Color:White"></input>
</th>
<th class="myclass" Style="color:Black;font-family:Tahoma;font-size:10px"
Align=Right nowrap>LoginUser:</TH>
<th>
<Input type='text' id=lnu style="width:150px;background-
Color:navy;Color:White"></input>
</TH>
<TH class="myclass" Style="color:Black;font-family:Tahoma;font-size:10px"
Align=Right nowrap>Password:</TH>
<TH>
<Input type='password' id=lpwd style="width:150px;background-
Color:navy;Color:White"></input>
</TH>
```

```
    <TH   class="myclass"   Style="color:Black;font-family:Tahoma;font-size:10px"
Align=Right nowrap>Your Mail Name:</TH>
    <TH>
    <Input      type='text'      id=emfn      style="width:150px;background-
Color:navy;Color:White"></input>
    </TH>
    </TR>
    <TR><TH   class="myclass"   Style="color:Black;font-family:Tahoma;font-
size:10px" Align=Right Nowrap>Your Mail Address:</TH>
    <th>
    <Input      type='text'      id=ema      style="width:150px;background-
Color:navy;Color:White"></input>
    </th>
    <th   class="myclass"   Style="color:Black;font-family:Tahoma;font-size:10px"
Align=Right nowrap>Sending it to:</TH>
    <th>
    <Input      type='text'      id="rec"      style="width:150px;background-
Color:navy;Color:White"></input>
    </TH>
    <TH   class="myclass"   Style="color:Black;font-family:Tahoma;font-size:10px"
Align=Right nowrap>Subject</TH>
    <TH colspan=4>
    <Input      type='text'      id=s      style="width:415px;background-
Color:navy;Color:White"></input>
    </TH>
    </TR>
    </table>


    <script language="vbscript">

    Dim cnstr
    Dim cn
    Dim Provider
    Dim rs

    Dim EngineConfiguration
    Dim HTMLEngineConfiguration
    Dim txtstream
    Dim TableType
```

```
Dim Orientation
Dim ControlType
Dim Filename
Dim strQuery
Dim Tablename
Dim Value
Dim StyleSheet


Provider="Microsoft.Jet.OleDb.3.51"

Filename = ""
strQuery = ""
Tablename = ""

EngineConfiguration = "rs"
HTMLEngineConfiguration = "rs"
TableType = "Table"
Orientation = "Multi-Line Horizontal"
ControlType = "Span"
StyleSheet = "InLine"

Sub Window_onLoad()

    window.moveTo 0, 0
    window.resizeTo 1055, 975
    RunMe.Disabled = true

End Sub

Sub HandlesEngineTypeChange()

    If EngineTypePullDown.Value <> "*Select An Option*" then

        EngineConfiguration = EngineTypePullDown.Value

    End If

End sub
```

```
Sub HandlesHTMLEngineTypeChange()

    If HTMLEngineTypePullDown.Value <> "*Select An Option*" then

        HTMLEngineConfiguration = HTMLEngineTypePullDown.Value

    End If

End sub

Sub st_OnClick()
    If st.Checked = true then
        dynamic.Checked = false
        cloaked.Checked = false
        bound.Checked = false
        If trexPullDown.Value <> "*Select An Option*" then
            Write_The_Code
        End If
    End If
End Sub

Sub dynamic_OnClick()
    If dynamic.Checked = true then
        st.Checked = false
        cloaked.Checked = false
        bound.Checked = false
        If trexPullDown.Value <> "*Select An Option*" then
            Write_The_Code
        End If
    End If
End Sub

Sub cloaked_OnClick()
    If cloaked.Checked = true then
        dynamic.Checked = false
        st.Checked = false
        bound.Checked = false
        If trexPullDown.Value <> "*Select An Option*" then
            Write_The_Code
        End If
```

```
        End If
End Sub

Sub bound_OnClick()
   If bound.Checked = true then
      dynamic.Checked = false
      cloaked.Checked = false
      st.Checked = false
      If trexPullDown.Value <> "*Select An Option*" then
         Write_The_Code
      End If
   End If
End Sub


Sub HandlesTableTypeChange()

   If TableTypePullDown.Value <> "*Select A TableType*" Then
      TableType = TableTypePullDown.Value
      Write_The_Code

   End If

End Sub


Sub HandlestrexChange()

   If trexPullDown.Value <> "*Select An Option*" then

      dim pos
      pos = instr(trexPullDown.Value, " ")
      if pos > 0 then
         CQuery.Value = "Select * From [" & trexPullDown.Value & "]"
      else
         CQuery.Value = "Select * From " & trexPullDown.Value
      End If

   End If
```

```
        End Sub


     Sub HandlesOrientationChange()

        If OrientationPullDown.Value <> "*Select An Orientation*" Then
          Orientation = OrientationPullDown.Value
          Write_The_Code
        End If

     End Sub

     Sub HandlesControlTypeChange()

        If ControlTypePullDown.Value <> "*Select An Additional Tag*" Then
          ControlType = ControlTypePullDown.Value
          Write_The_Code
        End If

     End Sub

     Sub HandlesStyleSheetChange()

     If StyleSheetPullDown.Value <> "*Select A StyleSheet*" Then
          StyleSheet = StyleSheetPullDown.Value
          Write_The_Code
     End If

     End Sub

     Sub Write_The_Code()

            textarea1.innerText = ""

        If FName.Value = "" then
             msgbox("Please provide the location and name of the database you want
to use before clicking here.")
             exit sub
        else
             Filename = FName.Value
```

```vb
    End If

    If CQuery.Value = "" then
        msgbox("Please create a Query string before clicking here.")
        exit sub
    End If

    strQuery = CQuery.Value

    dim pos
    pos = instr(trexPullDown.Value, " ")
    if pos > 0 then
        Tablename = Replace(trexPullDown.Value, " ", "_")
    else
        Tablename = trexPullDown.Value
    End If

    if st.Checked = True then
        Do_Static
        Exit Sub

    End If

    if dynamic.Checked = True then

        Do_Dynamic
        Exit Sub

    End If

    if cloaked.Checked = True then

        Do_Cloaked
        Exit Sub

    End If

    if bound.Checked = True then

        Do_Bound
```

```vb
        Exit Sub

    End If

End sub

Sub Do_Static()

    Select Case EngineConfiguration

        Case "cncmdrs"

            Set cn = CreateObject("ADODB.Connection")
            Set cmd = CreateObject("ADODB.Command")
            Set rs = CreateObject("ADODB.Recordset")

            cn.ConnectionString = "Provider=" & Provider & ";Data Source=" &
fName.Value & ";"
            Call cn.Open()

            cmd.ActiveConnection = cn
            cmd.CommandType = 8
            cmd.CommandText = strQuery
            Call cmd.Execute()

            rs.CursorLocation = 3
            rs.LockType = 3
            Call rs.Open(cmd)

        Case "cnrs"

            Set cn = CreateObject("ADODB.Connection")
            Set rs = CreateObject("ADODB.Recordset")
```

```vbscript
            cn.ConnectionString = "Provider=" & Provider & ";Data Source=" &
fName.Value & ";"
            Call cn.Open()

            rs.ActiveConnection = cn
            rs.CursorLocation = 3
            rs.LockType = 3
            rs.Source = strQuery
            Call rs.Open()

        Case "cmdrs"

            Set cmd = CreateObject("ADODB.Command")
            Set rs = CreateObject("ADODB.Recordset")

            cmd.ActiveConnection = "Provider=" & Provider & ";Data Source=" &
fName.Value & ";"
            cmd.CommandType = 8
            cmd.CommandText = strQuery
            Call cmd.Execute()

            rs.CursorLocation = 3
            rs.LockType = 3
            Call rs.Open(cmd)

        Case "rs"

            Set rs = CreateObject("ADODB.Recordset")
            rs.ActiveConnection = "Provider=" & Provider & ";Data Source=" &
fName.Value & ";"
            rs.LockType = 3
            rs.Cursorlocation = 3
            rs.Source = strQuery
            Call rs.Open()

    End Select


        Set ws = CreateObject("WScript.Shell")
```

```
Set fso = CreateObject("Scripting.FileSystemObject")

Set txtstream = fso.OpenTextFile(ws.CurrentDirectory & "\" & tablename &
".html", 2, True, -2)
txtstream.WriteLine("<html>")
txtstream.WriteLine("<head>")
txtstream.WriteLine("<title>" & Tablename & "</title>")

Add_The_StyleSheet

txtstream.WriteLine("</head>")
txtstream.WriteLine("<body>")
txtstream.WriteLine("")

If StyleSheet = "InLine" Then


Select Case Orientation


Case "Single-Line Horizontal"

Select Case TableType

Case "Table"

txtstream.WriteLine("<table        Border='1'      cellpadding='1'
cellspacing='1' datasrc=#rs>")

Case "Report"

txtstream.WriteLine("<table        Border='0'      cellpadding='1'
cellspacing='1' datasrc=#rs>")

End Select

txtstream.WriteLine("<tr>")
For x = 0 To rs.Fields.Count - 1
```

```
                txtstream.WriteLine("<th        style='font-family:Calibri,    Sans-
Serif;font-size: 12px;color:darkred;'>" & rs.Fields(x).Name & "</th>")


            Next
            txtstream.WriteLine("</tr>")
            txtstream.WriteLine("<tr>")
            For x = 0 To rs.Fields.Count - 1


                Select Case ControlType


                    Case "None"
                        txtstream.WriteLine("<td             style='font-
family:Calibri,  Sans-Serif;font-size:  12px;color:navy;'>"  &  rs.Fields(x).Value  &
"</td>")
                    Case "Button"
                        txtstream.WriteLine("<td             style='font-
family:Calibri, Sans-Serif;font-size: 12px;color:navy;'><input type=button Value='"
& rs.Fields(x).Value & "'></input></td>")
                    Case "Combobox"
                        txtstream.WriteLine("<td             style='font-
family:Calibri, Sans-Serif;font-size: 12px;color:navy;'><select><option Value='" &
rs.Fields(x).Value & "'>" & rs.Fields(x).Value & "</option></select></td>")
                    Case "Div"
                        txtstream.WriteLine("<td             style='font-
family:Calibri, Sans-Serif;font-size: 12px;color:navy;'><div>" & rs.Fields(x).Value &
"</div></td>")
                    Case "Listbox"
                        txtstream.WriteLine("<td             style='font-
family:Calibri,         Sans-Serif;font-size:          12px;color:navy;'><select
multiple=true><option Value ='" & rs.Fields(x).Value & "'>" & rs.Fields(x).Value &
"</option></select></td>")
                    Case "Span"
                        txtstream.WriteLine("<td             style='font-
family:Calibri, Sans-Serif;font-size: 12px;color:navy;'><span>" & rs.Fields(x).Value
& "</span></td>")
                    Case "Textbox"
                        txtstream.WriteLine("<td             style='font-
family:Calibri, Sans-Serif;font-size: 12px;color:navy;'><input type=text Value='" &
rs.Fields(x).Value & "'></input></td>")
```

```
                Case "Textarea"
                                    txtstream.WriteLine("<td              style='font-
family:Calibri,       Sans-Serif;font-size:      12px;color:navy;'><textarea>"      &
rs.Fields(x).Value & "</textarea></td>")

            End Select



            Next

            txtstream.WriteLine("</tr>")


        Case "Multi-Line Horizontal"


        Select Case TableType

            Case "Table"

                txtstream.WriteLine("<table        Border='1'      cellpadding='1'
cellspacing='1'>")

                Case "Report"

                txtstream.WriteLine("<table        Border='0'      cellpadding='1'
cellspacing='1'>")

            End Select

            txtstream.WriteLine("<tr>")
            For x = 0 To rs.Fields.Count - 1

                txtstream.WriteLine("<th       style='font-family:Calibri,      Sans-
Serif;font-size: 12px;color:darkred;'>" & rs.Fields(x).Name & "</th>")

            Next
            txtstream.WriteLine("</tr>")
            Do While rs.EOF = False
```

```vb
txtstream.WriteLine("<tr>")
For x = 0 To rs.Fields.Count - 1

    Select Case ControlType

        Case "None"
            txtstream.WriteLine("<td style='font-family:Calibri, Sans-Serif;font-size: 12px;color:navy;'>" & rs.Fields(x).Value & "</td>")
        Case "Button"
            txtstream.WriteLine("<td style='font-family:Calibri, Sans-Serif;font-size: 12px;color:navy;'><input type=button Value='" & rs.Fields(x).Value & "'></input></td>")
        Case "Combobox"
            txtstream.WriteLine("<td style='font-family:Calibri, Sans-Serif;font-size: 12px;color:navy;'><select><option Value='" & rs.Fields(x).Value & "'>" & rs.Fields(x).Value & "</option></select></td>")
        Case "Div"
            txtstream.WriteLine("<td style='font-family:Calibri, Sans-Serif;font-size: 12px;color:navy;'><div>" & rs.Fields(x).Value & "</div></td>")
        Case "Listbox"
            txtstream.WriteLine("<td style='font-family:Calibri, Sans-Serif;font-size: 12px;color:navy;'><select multiple=true><option Value ='" & rs.Fields(x).Value & "'>" & rs.Fields(x).Value & "</option></select></td>")
        Case "Span"
            txtstream.WriteLine("<td style='font-family:Calibri, Sans-Serif;font-size: 12px;color:navy;'><span>" & rs.Fields(x).Value & "</span></td>")
        Case "Textbox"
            txtstream.WriteLine("<td style='font-family:Calibri, Sans-Serif;font-size: 12px;color:navy;'><input type=text Value='" & rs.Fields(x).Value & "'></input></td>")
        Case "Textarea"
            txtstream.WriteLine("<td style='font-family:Calibri, Sans-Serif;font-size: 12px;color:navy;'><textarea>" & rs.Fields(x).Value & "</textarea></td>")
```

```vb
            End Select


        Next
        txtstream.WriteLine("</tr>")
        rs.MoveNext()
    Loop



Case "Single-Line Vertical"


    Select Case TableType

        Case "Table"

            txtstream.WriteLine("<table        Border='1'      cellpadding='1'
cellspacing='1'>")

        Case "Report"

            txtstream.WriteLine("<table        Border='0'      cellpadding='1'
cellspacing='1'>")

    End Select

    For x = 0 To rs.Fields.Count - 1

    Select Case ControlType

        Case "None"
            txtstream.WriteLine("<tr><th          style='font-
family:Calibri, Sans-Serif;font-size: 12px;color:darkred;'>" & rs.Fields(x).Name &
"</th><td style='font-family:Calibri, Sans-Serif;font-size: 12px;color:navy;'>" &
rs.Fields(x).Value & "</td></tr>")
        Case "Button"
            txtstream.WriteLine("<tr><th          style='font-
family:Calibri, Sans-Serif;font-size: 12px;color:darkred;'>" & rs.Fields(x).Name &
```

```
"</th><td style='font-family:Calibri, Sans-Serif;font-size: 12px;color:navy;'><input
type=button Value='" & rs.Fields(x).Value & "'></input></td></tr>")
                    Case "Combobox"
                        txtstream.WriteLine("<tr><th          style='font-
family:Calibri, Sans-Serif;font-size: 12px;color:darkred;'>" & rs.Fields(x).Name &
"</th>        <td          style='font-family:Calibri,      Sans-Serif;font-size:
12px;color:navy;'><select><option  Value='"  &  rs.Fields(x).Value  &  "'>"  &
rs.Fields(x).Value & "</option></select></td></tr>")
                    Case "Div"
                        txtstream.WriteLine("<tr><th          style='font-
family:Calibri, Sans-Serif;font-size: 12px;color:darkred;'>" & rs.Fields(x).Name &
"</th><td style='font-family:Calibri, Sans-Serif;font-size: 12px;color:navy;'><div>"
& rs.Fields(x).Value & "</div></td></tr>")
                    Case "Listbox"
                        txtstream.WriteLine("<tr><th          style='font-
family:Calibri, Sans-Serif;font-size: 12px;color:darkred;'>" & rs.Fields(x).Name &
"</th><td style='font-family:Calibri, Sans-Serif;font-size: 12px;color:navy;'><select
multiple=true><option Value ='" & rs.Fields(x).Value & "'>" & rs.Fields(x).Value &
"</option></select></td></tr>")
                    Case "Span"
                        txtstream.WriteLine("<tr><th          style='font-
family:Calibri, Sans-Serif;font-size: 12px;color:darkred;'>" & rs.Fields(x).Name &
"</th><td          style='font-family:Calibri,          Sans-Serif;font-size:
12px;color:navy;'><span>" & rs.Fields(x).Value & "</span></td></tr>")
                    Case "Textbox"
                        txtstream.WriteLine("<tr><th          style='font-
family:Calibri, Sans-Serif;font-size: 12px;color:darkred;'>" & rs.Fields(x).Name &
"</th><td style='font-family:Calibri, Sans-Serif;font-size: 12px;color:navy;'><input
type=text Value='" & rs.Fields(x).Value & "'></input></td></tr>")
                    Case "Textarea"
                        txtstream.WriteLine("<tr><th          style='font-
family:Calibri, Sans-Serif;font-size: 12px;color:darkred;'>" & rs.Fields(x).Name &
"</th><td          style='font-family:Calibri,          Sans-Serif;font-size:
12px;color:navy;'><textarea>" & rs.Fields(x).Value & "</textarea></td></tr>")


                End Select


            Next
```

```
Case "Multi-Line Vertical"

    Select Case TableType

        Case "Table"

            txtstream.WriteLine("<table        Border='1'        cellpadding='1'
cellspacing='1'>")

        Case "Report"

            txtstream.WriteLine("<table        Border='0'        cellpadding='1'
cellspacing='1'>")

    End Select


    For x = 0 To rs.Fields.Count - 1

        txtstream.WriteLine("<tr><th   style='font-family:Calibri,   Sans-
Serif;font-size: 12px;color:darkred;'>" & rs.Fields(x).Name & "</th>")

    rs.MoveFirst()

    Do While rs.EOF = False


        Select Case ControlType

            Case "None"
                            txtstream.WriteLine("<td   style='font-
family:Calibri,  Sans-Serif;font-size:  12px;color:navy;'>" &  rs.Fields(x).Value  &
"</td>")
            Case "Button"
                            txtstream.WriteLine("<td   style='font-
family:Calibri, Sans-Serif;font-size: 12px;color:navy;'><input type=button Value='"
& rs.Fields(x).Value & "'></input></td>")
            Case "Combobox"
```

```vb
                    txtstream.WriteLine("<td    style='font-
family:Calibri, Sans-Serif;font-size: 12px;color:navy;'><select><option Value='" &
rs.Fields(x).Value & "'>" & rs.Fields(x).Value & "</option></select></td>")
                Case "Div"

                    txtstream.WriteLine("<td    style='font-
family:Calibri, Sans-Serif;font-size: 12px;color:navy;'><div>" & rs.Fields(x).Value &
"</div></td>")
                Case "Listbox"

                    txtstream.WriteLine("<td    style='font-
family:Calibri,          Sans-Serif;font-size:          12px;color:navy;'><select
multiple=true><option Value ='" & rs.Fields(x).Value & "'>" & rs.Fields(x).Value &
"</option></select></td>")
                Case "Span"

                    txtstream.WriteLine("<td    style='font-
family:Calibri, Sans-Serif;font-size: 12px;color:navy;'><span>" & rs.Fields(x).Value
& "</span></td>")
                Case "Textbox"

                    txtstream.WriteLine("<td    style='font-
family:Calibri, Sans-Serif;font-size: 12px;color:navy;'><input type=text Value='" &
rs.Fields(x).Value & "'></input></td>")
                Case "Textarea"

                    txtstream.WriteLine("<td    style='font-
family:Calibri,     Sans-Serif;font-size:     12px;color:navy;'><textarea>"     &
rs.Fields(x).Value & "</textarea></td>")

            End Select

            rs.MoveNext()

        Loop

        txtstream.WriteLine("</tr>")

    Next


    End Select
```

```
        Else

            Select Case Orientation

                Case "Single-Line Horizontal"

                    Select Case TableType

                        Case "Table"

                            txtstream.WriteLine("<table        Border='1'       cellpadding='1'
cellspacing='1' datasrc=#rs>")

                        Case "Report"

                            txtstream.WriteLine("<table        Border='0'       cellpadding='1'
cellspacing='1' datasrc=#rs>")

                    End Select


                    txtstream.WriteLine("<tr>")
                    For x = 0 To rs.Fields.Count - 1

                        txtstream.WriteLine("<th>" & rs.Fields(x).Name & "</th>")

                    Next
                    txtstream.WriteLine("</tr>")
                    txtstream.WriteLine("<tr>")
                    For x = 0 To rs.Fields.Count - 1


                        Select Case ControlType

                            Case "None"
                                        txtstream.WriteLine("<td>" & rs.Fields(x).Value
& "</td>")
                            Case "Button"
```

```vb
                                txtstream.WriteLine("<td><input    type=button
Value='" & rs.Fields(x).Value & "'></input></td>")
                        Case "Combobox"

                                txtstream.WriteLine("<td><select><option
Value='"      &      rs.Fields(x).Value      &      "'>"      &      rs.Fields(x).Value      &
"</option></select></td>")
                        Case "Div"

                                txtstream.WriteLine("<td><div>"                        &
rs.Fields(x).Value & "</div></td>")
                        Case "Listbox"

                                txtstream.WriteLine("<td><select
multiple=true><option Value ='" & rs.Fields(x).Value & "'>" & rs.Fields(x).Value &
"</option></select></td>")
                        Case "Span"

                                txtstream.WriteLine("<td><span>"                        &
rs.Fields(x).Value & "</span></td>")
                        Case "Textbox"

                                txtstream.WriteLine("<td><input       type=text
Value='" & rs.Fields(x).Value & "'></input></td>")
                        Case "Textarea"

                                txtstream.WriteLine("<td><textarea>"                    &
rs.Fields(x).Value & "</textarea></td>")


                End Select



                Next


        txtstream.WriteLine("</tr>")


        Case "Multi-Line Horizontal"


        Select Case TableType

                Case "Table"
```

```
                    txtstream.WriteLine("<table        Border='1'      cellpadding='1'
cellspacing='1'>")

              Case "Report"

                    txtstream.WriteLine("<table        Border='0'      cellpadding='1'
cellspacing='1'>")

              End Select

              txtstream.WriteLine("<tr>")
              For x = 0 To rs.Fields.Count - 1

                 txtstream.WriteLine("<th>" & rs.Fields(x).Name & "</th>")

              Next
              txtstream.WriteLine("</tr>")
              Do While rs.EOF = False

                  '
                 txtstream.WriteLine("<tr>")
                 For x = 0 To rs.Fields.Count - 1

                    Select Case ControlType

                       Case "None"
                                       txtstream.WriteLine("<td>"             &
rs.Fields(x).Value & "</td>")
                       Case "Button"
                                       txtstream.WriteLine("<td><input
type=button Value='" & rs.Fields(x).Value & "'></input></td>")
                       Case "Combobox"

                 txtstream.WriteLine("<td><select><option Value='" & rs.Fields(x).Value &
"'>" & rs.Fields(x).Value & "</option></select></td>")
                       Case "Div"
                                       txtstream.WriteLine("<td><div>"        &
rs.Fields(x).Value & "</div></td>")
                       Case "Listbox"
```

```vb
                                    txtstream.WriteLine("<td><select
multiple=true><option Value ='" & rs.Fields(x).Value & "'>" & rs.Fields(x).Value &
"</option></select></td>")
                Case "Span"

                                    txtstream.WriteLine("<td><span>"       &
rs.Fields(x).Value & "</span></td>")
                Case "Textbox"

                                    txtstream.WriteLine("<td><input
type=text Value='" & rs.Fields(x).Value & "'></input></td>")
                Case "Textarea"

                                    txtstream.WriteLine("<td><textarea>"
& rs.Fields(x).Value & "</textarea></td>")


            End Select



        Next
        txtstream.WriteLine("</tr>")
        rs.MoveNext()
    Loop



        Case "Single-Line Vertical"



        Select Case TableType

        Case "Table"

                    txtstream.WriteLine("<table       Border='1'      cellpadding='1'
cellspacing='1'>")

        Case "Report"

                    txtstream.WriteLine("<table       Border='0'      cellpadding='1'
cellspacing='1'>")

        End Select
```

```
For x = 0 To rs.Fields.Count - 1

    Select Case ControlType

        Case "None"
                    txtstream.WriteLine("<tr><th>"                    &
rs.Fields(x).Name & "</th><td>" & rs.Fields(x).Value & "</td></tr>")
        Case "Button"
                    txtstream.WriteLine("<tr><th>"                    &
rs.Fields(x).Name & "</th><td><input type=button Value='" & rs.Fields(x).Value &
"'></input></td></tr>")
        Case "Combobox"
                    txtstream.WriteLine("<tr><th>"                    &
rs.Fields(x).Name & "</th> <td><select><option Value='" & rs.Fields(x).Value &
"'>" & rs.Fields(x).Value & "</option></select></td></tr>")
        Case "Div"
                    txtstream.WriteLine("<tr><th>"                    &
rs.Fields(x).Name & "</th><td><div>" & rs.Fields(x).Value & "</div></td></tr>")
        Case "Listbox"
                    txtstream.WriteLine("<tr><th>"                    &
rs.Fields(x).Name  &  "</th><td><select  multiple=true><option  Value ='"  &
rs.Fields(x).Value & "'>" & rs.Fields(x).Value & "</option></select></td></tr>")
        Case "Span"
                    txtstream.WriteLine("<tr><th>"                    &
rs.Fields(x).Name     &     "</th><td><span>"     &     rs.Fields(x).Value     &
"</span></td></tr>")
        Case "Textbox"
                    txtstream.WriteLine("<tr><th>"                    &
rs.Fields(x).Name & "</th><td><input type=text Value='" & rs.Fields(x).Value &
"'></input></td></tr>")
        Case "Textarea"
                    txtstream.WriteLine("<tr><th>"                    &
rs.Fields(x).Name     &     "</th><td><textarea>"     &     rs.Fields(x).Value     &
"</textarea></td></tr>")

    End Select

Next
```

```
        Case "Multi-Line Vertical"

            Select Case TableType

                Case "Table"

                        txtstream.WriteLine("<table     Border='1'     cellpadding='1'
cellspacing='1'>")

                    Case "Report"

                        txtstream.WriteLine("<table     Border='0'     cellpadding='1'
cellspacing='1'>")

                End Select


            For x = 0 To rs.Fields.Count - 1

                txtstream.WriteLine("<tr><th>" & rs.Fields(x).Name & "</th>")

                rs.MoveFirst()

                Do While rs.EOF = False


                    Select Case ControlType

                        Case "None"
                                            txtstream.WriteLine("<td>"           &
rs.Fields(x).Value & "</td>")
                        Case "Button"
                                            txtstream.WriteLine("<td><input
type=button Value='" & rs.Fields(x).Value & "'></input></td>")
                        Case "Combobox"

            txtstream.WriteLine("<td><select><option Value='" & rs.Fields(x).Value &
"'>" & rs.Fields(x).Value & "</option></select></td>")
                        Case "Div"
```

```
                              txtstream.WriteLine("<td><div>"        &
rs.Fields(x).Value & "</div></td>")
                Case "Listbox"

                              txtstream.WriteLine("<td><select
multiple=true><option Value ='" & rs.Fields(x).Value & "'>" & rs.Fields(x).Value &
"</option></select></td>")
                Case "Span"

                              txtstream.WriteLine("<td><span>"       &
rs.Fields(x).Value & "</span></td>")
                Case "Textbox"

                              txtstream.WriteLine("<td><input
type=text Value='" & rs.Fields(x).Value & "'></input></td>")
                Case "Textarea"

                              txtstream.WriteLine("<td><textarea>"
& rs.Fields(x).Value & "</textarea></td>")

        End Select

        rs.MoveNext()

    Loop

    txtstream.WriteLine("</tr>")

    Next


    End Select


    End If

    txtstream.WriteLine("</table>")
    txtstream.WriteLine("</body>")
    txtstream.WriteLine("</html>")
    txtstream.Close
```

```vbscript
        tempstr = ""
        Set txtstream = fso.OpenTextFile(ws.CurrentDirectory & "\" & Tablename &
".html", 1, true, -2)
        Do While txtstream.AtEndOfStream = false
           tempstr = tempstr & txtstream.ReadLine()
           tempstr = tempstr & vbcrlf
        loop
        txtstream.Close
        textarea1.innerText = tempstr


End Sub

Sub Do_Dynamic()

    Select Case EngineConfiguration


        Case "cncmdrs"


                Set cn = CreateObject("ADODB.Connection")
                Set cmd = CreateObject("ADODB.Command")
                Set rs = CreateObject("ADODB.Recordset")


                cn.ConnectionString = "Provider=" & Provider & ";Data Source=" &
fName.Value & ";"
                Call cn.Open()

                cmd.ActiveConnection = cn
                cmd.CommandType = 8
                cmd.CommandText = strQuery
                Call cmd.Execute()

                rs.CursorLocation = 3
                rs.LockType = 3
                Call rs.Open(cmd)
```

```
Case "cnrs"

        Set cn = CreateObject("ADODB.Connection")
        Set rs = CreateObject("ADODB.Recordset")

        cn.ConnectionString = "Provider=" & Provider & ";Data Source=" &
fName.Value & ";"
        Call cn.Open()

        rs.ActiveConnection = cn
        rs.CursorLocation = 3
        rs.LockType = 3
        rs.Source = strQuery
        Call rs.Open()

Case "cmdrs"

        Set cmd = CreateObject("ADODB.Command")
        Set rs = CreateObject("ADODB.Recordset")

        cmd.ActiveConnection = "Provider=" & Provider & ";Data Source=" &
fName.Value & ";"
        cmd.CommandType = 8
        cmd.CommandText = strQuery
        Call cmd.Execute()

        rs.CursorLocation = 3
        rs.LockType = 3
        Call rs.Open(cmd)

Case "rs"

        Set rs = CreateObject("ADODB.Recordset")
        rs.ActiveConnection = "Provider=" & Provider & ";Data Source=" &
fName.Value & ";"
        rs.LockType = 3
        rs.Cursorlocation = 3
        rs.Source = strQuery
        Call rs.Open()
```

```
        End Select

            Set ws = CreateObject("WScript.Shell")
            Set fso = CreateObject("Scripting.FileSystemObject")

            Set txtstream = fso.OpenTextFile(ws.CurrentDirectory & "\" & Tablename &
    ".html", 2, True, -2)
            txtstream.WriteLine ("<html>")
            txtstream.WriteLine ("<head>")
            txtstream.WriteLine ("<title>" & Tablename & "</title>")

        Add_The_StyleSheet

            txtstream.WriteLine ("</head>")
            txtstream.WriteLine ("<body>")
            txtstream.WriteLine ("<script language='vbscript'>")

        If StyleSheet = "InLine" Then


            Select Case Orientation


                Case "Single-Line Horizontal"

                    Select Case TableType

                        Case "Table"

                            txtstream.WriteLine  ("document.WriteLn(""<table  Border='1'
    cellpadding='1' cellspacing='1' datasrc=#rs>"")")

                        Case "Report"

                            txtstream.WriteLine  ("document.WriteLn(""<table  Border='0'
    cellpadding='1' cellspacing='1' datasrc=#rs>"")")

                    End Select
```

```
txtstream.WriteLine ("document.WriteLn(""<tr>"")")
For x = 0 To rs.Fields.Count - 1

    txtstream.WriteLine    ("document.WriteLn(""<th    style='font-
family:Calibri, Sans-Serif;font-size: 12px;color:darkred;'>" & rs.Fields(x).Name &
"</th>"")")

Next
txtstream.WriteLine ("document.WriteLn(""</tr>"")")
txtstream.WriteLine ("document.WriteLn(""<tr>"")")
For x = 0 To rs.Fields.Count - 1


    Select Case ControlType

        Case "None"
        txtstream.WriteLine    ("document.WriteLn(""<td    style='font-
family:Calibri, Sans-Serif;font-size: 12px;color:navy;'>" & rs.Fields(x).Value &
"</td>"")")
        Case "Button"
        txtstream.WriteLine    ("document.WriteLn(""<td    style='font-
family:Calibri, Sans-Serif;font-size: 12px;color:navy;'><input type=button Value='"
& rs.Fields(x).Value & "'></input></td>"")")
        Case "Combobox"
        txtstream.WriteLine    ("document.WriteLn(""<td    style='font-
family:Calibri, Sans-Serif;font-size: 12px;color:navy;'><select><option Value='" &
rs.Fields(x).Value & "'>" & rs.Fields(x).Value & "</option></select></td>"")")
        Case "Div"
        txtstream.WriteLine    ("document.WriteLn(""<td    style='font-
family:Calibri, Sans-Serif;font-size: 12px;color:navy;'><div>" & rs.Fields(x).Value &
"</div></td>"")")
        Case "Listbox"
        txtstream.WriteLine    ("document.WriteLn(""<td    style='font-
family:Calibri,        Sans-Serif;font-size:        12px;color:navy;'><select
multiple=true><option Value ='" & rs.Fields(x).Value & "'>" & rs.Fields(x).Value &
"</option></select></td>"")")
        Case "Span"
        txtstream.WriteLine    ("document.WriteLn(""<td    style='font-
family:Calibri, Sans-Serif;font-size: 12px;color:navy;'><span>" & rs.Fields(x).Value
& "</span></td>"")")
```

```
                Case "Textbox"
            txtstream.WriteLine        ("document.WriteLn(""<td        style='font-
family:Calibri, Sans-Serif;font-size: 12px;color:navy;'><input type=text Value='" &
rs.Fields(x).Value & "'></input></td>""")")
                Case "Textarea"
            txtstream.WriteLine        ("document.WriteLn(""<td        style='font-
family:Calibri,     Sans-Serif;font-size:     12px;color:navy;'><textarea>"     &
rs.Fields(x).Value & "</textarea></td>""")")

            End Select



        Next


        txtstream.WriteLine ("document.WriteLn(""</tr>""")")


    Case "Multi-Line Horizontal"


    Select Case TableType

        Case "Table"

            txtstream.WriteLine   ("document.WriteLn(""<table   Border='1'
cellpadding='1' cellspacing='1'>""")")

        Case "Report"

            txtstream.WriteLine   ("document.WriteLn(""<table   Border='0'
cellpadding='1' cellspacing='1'>""")")

    End Select

    txtstream.WriteLine ("document.WriteLn(""<tr>""")")
    For x = 0 To rs.Fields.Count - 1
```

```
            txtstream.WriteLine      ("document.WriteLn(""<th      style='font-
family:Calibri, Sans-Serif;font-size: 12px;color:darkred;'>" & rs.Fields(x).Name &
"</th>""")")

        Next
        txtstream.WriteLine ("document.WriteLn(""</tr>""")")
        Do While rs.EOF = False

        txtstream.WriteLine ("document.WriteLn(""<tr>""")")
        For x = 0 To rs.Fields.Count - 1

        Select Case ControlType

            Case "None"
            txtstream.WriteLine      ("document.WriteLn(""<td      style='font-
family:Calibri, Sans-Serif;font-size: 12px;color:navy;'>" & rs.Fields(x).Value &
"</td>""")")
            Case "Button"
            txtstream.WriteLine      ("document.WriteLn(""<td      style='font-
family:Calibri, Sans-Serif;font-size: 12px;color:navy;'><input type=button Value='"
& rs.Fields(x).Value & "'></input></td>""")")
            Case "Combobox"
            txtstream.WriteLine      ("document.WriteLn(""<td      style='font-
family:Calibri, Sans-Serif;font-size: 12px;color:navy;'><select><option Value='" &
rs.Fields(x).Value & "'>" & rs.Fields(x).Value & "</option></select></td>""")")
            Case "Div"
            txtstream.WriteLine      ("document.WriteLn(""<td      style='font-
family:Calibri, Sans-Serif;font-size: 12px;color:navy;'><div>" & rs.Fields(x).Value &
"</div></td>""")")
            Case "Listbox"
            txtstream.WriteLine      ("document.WriteLn(""<td      style='font-
family:Calibri,          Sans-Serif;font-size:          12px;color:navy;'><select
multiple=true><option Value ='" & rs.Fields(x).Value & "'>" & rs.Fields(x).Value &
"</option></select></td>""")")
            Case "Span"
            txtstream.WriteLine      ("document.WriteLn(""<td      style='font-
family:Calibri, Sans-Serif;font-size: 12px;color:navy;'><span>" & rs.Fields(x).Value
& "</span></td>""")")
            Case "Textbox"
```

```
            txtstream.WriteLine        ("document.WriteLn("""<td        style='font-
family:Calibri, Sans-Serif;font-size: 12px;color:navy;'><input type=text Value='" &
rs.Fields(x).Value & "'></input></td>""")")
                    Case "Textarea"
            txtstream.WriteLine        ("document.WriteLn("""<td        style='font-
family:Calibri,       Sans-Serif;font-size:       12px;color:navy;'><textarea>"       &
rs.Fields(x).Value & "</textarea></td>""")")

                End Select


            Next
            txtstream.WriteLine ("document.WriteLn("""</tr>""")")
            rs.MoveNext
        Loop



        Case "Single-Line Vertical"


        Select Case TableType

            Case "Table"

                txtstream.WriteLine    ("document.WriteLn("""<table    Border='1'
cellpadding='1' cellspacing='1'>""")")

            Case "Report"

                txtstream.WriteLine    ("document.WriteLn("""<table    Border='0'
cellpadding='1' cellspacing='1'>""")")

        End Select

        For x = 0 To rs.Fields.Count - 1

            Select Case ControlType

                Case "None"
```

```
        txtstream.WriteLine    ("document.WriteLn(""<tr><th    style='font-
family:Calibri, Sans-Serif;font-size: 12px;color:darkred;'>" & rs.Fields(x).Name &
"</th><td style='font-family:Calibri, Sans-Serif;font-size: 12px;color:navy;'>" &
rs.Fields(x).Value & "</td></tr>""")")
        Case "Button"
        txtstream.WriteLine    ("document.WriteLn(""<tr><th    style='font-
family:Calibri, Sans-Serif;font-size: 12px;color:darkred;'>" & rs.Fields(x).Name &
"</th><td style='font-family:Calibri, Sans-Serif;font-size: 12px;color:navy;'><input
type=button Value='" & rs.Fields(x).Value & "'></input></td></tr>""")")
        Case "Combobox"
        txtstream.WriteLine    ("document.WriteLn(""<tr><th    style='font-
family:Calibri, Sans-Serif;font-size: 12px;color:darkred;'>" & rs.Fields(x).Name &
"</th>       <td       style='font-family:Calibri,       Sans-Serif;font-size:
12px;color:navy;'><select><option  Value='"  &  rs.Fields(x).Value  &  "'>"  &
rs.Fields(x).Value & "</option></select></td></tr>""")")
        Case "Div"
        txtstream.WriteLine    ("document.WriteLn(""<tr><th    style='font-
family:Calibri, Sans-Serif;font-size: 12px;color:darkred;'>" & rs.Fields(x).Name &
"</th><td style='font-family:Calibri, Sans-Serif;font-size: 12px;color:navy;'><div>"
& rs.Fields(x).Value & "</div></td></tr>""")")
        Case "Listbox"
        txtstream.WriteLine    ("document.WriteLn(""<tr><th    style='font-
family:Calibri, Sans-Serif;font-size: 12px;color:darkred;'>" & rs.Fields(x).Name &
"</th><td style='font-family:Calibri, Sans-Serif;font-size: 12px;color:navy;'><select
multiple=true><option Value ='" & rs.Fields(x).Value & "'>" & rs.Fields(x).Value &
"</option></select></td></tr>""")")
        Case "Span"
        txtstream.WriteLine    ("document.WriteLn(""<tr><th    style='font-
family:Calibri, Sans-Serif;font-size: 12px;color:darkred;'>" & rs.Fields(x).Name &
"</th><td         style='font-family:Calibri,         Sans-Serif;font-size:
12px;color:navy;'><span>" & rs.Fields(x).Value & "</span></td></tr>""")")
        Case "Textbox"
        txtstream.WriteLine    ("document.WriteLn(""<tr><th    style='font-
family:Calibri, Sans-Serif;font-size: 12px;color:darkred;'>" & rs.Fields(x).Name &
"</th><td style='font-family:Calibri, Sans-Serif;font-size: 12px;color:navy;'><input
type=text Value='" & rs.Fields(x).Value & "'></input></td></tr>""")")
        Case "Textarea"
        txtstream.WriteLine    ("document.WriteLn(""<tr><th    style='font-
family:Calibri, Sans-Serif;font-size: 12px;color:darkred;'>" & rs.Fields(x).Name &
```

```
"</th><td                     style='font-family:Calibri,          Sans-Serif;font-size:
12px;color:navy;'><textarea>" & rs.Fields(x).Value & "</textarea></td></tr>""")")

            End Select

        Next


        Case "Multi-Line Vertical"


            Select Case TableType

                Case "Table"

                        txtstream.WriteLine    ("document.WriteLn(""""<table   Border='1'
cellpadding='1' cellspacing='1'>""")")

                Case "Report"

                        txtstream.WriteLine    ("document.WriteLn(""""<table   Border='0'
cellpadding='1' cellspacing='1'>""")")

            End Select


            For x = 0 To rs.Fields.Count - 1

                        txtstream.WriteLine   ("document.WriteLn(""""<tr><th style='font-
family:Calibri, Sans-Serif;font-size: 12px;color:darkred;'>" & rs.Fields(x).Name &
"</th>""")")

                rs.MoveFirst

            Do While rs.EOF = False


                Select Case ControlType

                    Case "None"
```

```
            txtstream.WriteLine      ("document.WriteLn(""<td      style='font-
family:Calibri,  Sans-Serif;font-size:  12px;color:navy;'>" & rs.Fields(x).Value &
"</td>"")")
                  Case "Button"
            txtstream.WriteLine      ("document.WriteLn(""<td      style='font-
family:Calibri, Sans-Serif;font-size: 12px;color:navy;'><input type=button Value='"
& rs.Fields(x).Value & "'></input></td>"")")
                  Case "Combobox"
            txtstream.WriteLine      ("document.WriteLn(""<td      style='font-
family:Calibri, Sans-Serif;font-size: 12px;color:navy;'><select><option Value='" &
rs.Fields(x).Value & "'>" & rs.Fields(x).Value & "</option></select></td>"")")
                  Case "Div"
            txtstream.WriteLine      ("document.WriteLn(""<td      style='font-
family:Calibri, Sans-Serif;font-size: 12px;color:navy;'><div>" & rs.Fields(x).Value &
"</div></td>"")")
                  Case "Listbox"
            txtstream.WriteLine      ("document.WriteLn(""<td      style='font-
family:Calibri,        Sans-Serif;font-size:        12px;color:navy;'><select
multiple=true><option Value ='" & rs.Fields(x).Value & "'>" & rs.Fields(x).Value &
"</option></select></td>"")")
                  Case "Span"
            txtstream.WriteLine      ("document.WriteLn(""<td      style='font-
family:Calibri, Sans-Serif;font-size: 12px;color:navy;'><span>" & rs.Fields(x).Value
& "</span></td>"")")
                  Case "Textbox"
            txtstream.WriteLine      ("document.WriteLn(""<td      style='font-
family:Calibri, Sans-Serif;font-size: 12px;color:navy;'><input type=text Value='" &
rs.Fields(x).Value & "'></input></td>"")")
                  Case "Textarea"
            txtstream.WriteLine      ("document.WriteLn(""<td      style='font-
family:Calibri,    Sans-Serif;font-size:    12px;color:navy;'><textarea>"    &
rs.Fields(x).Value & "</textarea></td>"")")

         End Select

         rs.MoveNext

      Loop

      txtstream.WriteLine ("document.WriteLn(""</tr>"")")
```

Next

End Select

Else

Select Case Orientation

Case "Single-Line Horizontal"

Select Case TableType

Case "Table"

txtstream.WriteLine ("document.WriteLn("""<table Border='1' cellpadding='1' cellspacing='1' datasrc=#rs>""")")

Case "Report"

txtstream.WriteLine ("document.WriteLn("""<table Border='0' cellpadding='1' cellspacing='1' datasrc=#rs>""")")

End Select

txtstream.WriteLine ("document.WriteLn("""<tr>""")")
For x = 0 To rs.Fields.Count - 1

txtstream.WriteLine ("document.WriteLn("""<th>" & rs.Fields(x).Name & "</th>""")")

Next
txtstream.WriteLine ("document.WriteLn("""</tr>""")")
txtstream.WriteLine ("document.WriteLn("""<tr>""")")

```vb
For x = 0 To rs.Fields.Count - 1


        Select Case ControlType

            Case "None"
            txtstream.WriteLine ("document.WriteLn("""<td>" & rs.Fields(x).Value
& "</td>""")")
            Case "Button"
            txtstream.WriteLine ("document.WriteLn("""<td><input type=button
Value='" & rs.Fields(x).Value & "'></input></td>""")")
            Case "Combobox"
            txtstream.WriteLine          ("document.WriteLn("""<td><select><option
Value='"      &     rs.Fields(x).Value     &     "'>"     &     rs.Fields(x).Value     &
"</option></select></td>""")")
            Case "Div"
            txtstream.WriteLine          ("document.WriteLn("""<td><div>"          &
rs.Fields(x).Value & "</div></td>""")")
            Case "Listbox"
            txtstream.WriteLine                    ("document.WriteLn("""<td><select
multiple=true><option Value ='" & rs.Fields(x).Value & "'>" & rs.Fields(x).Value &
"</option></select></td>""")")
            Case "Span"
            txtstream.WriteLine          ("document.WriteLn("""<td><span>"          &
rs.Fields(x).Value & "</span></td>""")")
            Case "Textbox"
            txtstream.WriteLine          ("document.WriteLn("""<td><input     type=text
Value='" & rs.Fields(x).Value & "'></input></td>""")")
            Case "Textarea"
            txtstream.WriteLine          ("document.WriteLn("""<td><textarea>"          &
rs.Fields(x).Value & "</textarea></td>""")")


        End Select


    Next

    txtstream.WriteLine ("document.WriteLn("""</tr>""")")
```

```vb
            Case "Multi-Line Horizontal"

                Select Case TableType

                    Case "Table"

                        txtstream.WriteLine   ("document.WriteLn(""<table  Border='1'
cellpadding='1' cellspacing='1'>"")")

                    Case "Report"

                        txtstream.WriteLine   ("document.WriteLn(""<table  Border='0'
cellpadding='1' cellspacing='1'>"")")

                End Select

                txtstream.WriteLine ("document.WriteLn(""<tr>"")")
                For x = 0 To rs.Fields.Count - 1

                        txtstream.WriteLine          ("document.WriteLn(""<th>"         &
rs.Fields(x).Name & "</th>"")")

                Next
                txtstream.WriteLine ("document.WriteLn(""</tr>"")")
                Do While rs.EOF = False

                    txtstream.WriteLine ("document.WriteLn(""<tr>"")")
                    For x = 0 To rs.Fields.Count - 1

                        Select Case ControlType

                            Case "None"
                        txtstream.WriteLine          ("document.WriteLn(""<td>"         &
rs.Fields(x).Value & "</td>"")")
                            Case "Button"
                        txtstream.WriteLine ("document.WriteLn(""<td><input type=button
Value='" & rs.Fields(x).Value & "'></input></td>"")")
                            Case "Combobox"
```

```
                txtstream.WriteLine        ("document.WriteLn(""<td><select><option
Value='"    &    rs.Fields(x).Value    &    "'>"    &    rs.Fields(x).Value    &
"</option></select></td>"")")
                        Case "Div"
                txtstream.WriteLine        ("document.WriteLn(""<td><div>"        &
rs.Fields(x).Value & "</div></td>"")")
                        Case "Listbox"
                txtstream.WriteLine               ("document.WriteLn(""<td><select
multiple=true><option Value ='" & rs.Fields(x).Value & "'>" & rs.Fields(x).Value &
"</option></select></td>"")")
                        Case "Span"
                txtstream.WriteLine        ("document.WriteLn(""<td><span>"        &
rs.Fields(x).Value & "</span></td>"")")
                        Case "Textbox"
                txtstream.WriteLine   ("document.WriteLn(""<td><input   type=text
Value='" & rs.Fields(x).Value & "'></input></td>"")")
                        Case "Textarea"
                txtstream.WriteLine    ("document.WriteLn(""<td><textarea>"       &
rs.Fields(x).Value & "</textarea></td>"")")


            End Select


        Next
        txtstream.WriteLine ("document.WriteLn(""</tr>"")")
        rs.MoveNext
    Loop



    Case "Single-Line Vertical"


      Select Case TableType


        Case "Table"


                txtstream.WriteLine   ("document.WriteLn(""<table   Border='1'
cellpadding='1' cellspacing='1'>"")")
```

```vb
                Case "Report"

                        txtstream.WriteLine  ("document.WriteLn(""""<table  Border='0'
cellpadding='1' cellspacing='1'>""")")

                End Select

                For x = 0 To rs.Fields.Count - 1

                Select Case ControlType

                        Case "None"
                txtstream.WriteLine          ("document.WriteLn(""""<tr><th>"          &
rs.Fields(x).Name & "</th><td>" & rs.Fields(x).Value & "</td></tr>""")")
                        Case "Button"
                txtstream.WriteLine          ("document.WriteLn(""""<tr><th>"          &
rs.Fields(x).Name & "</th><td><input type=button Value='" & rs.Fields(x).Value &
"'></input></td></tr>""")")
                        Case "Combobox"
                txtstream.WriteLine          ("document.WriteLn(""""<tr><th>"          &
rs.Fields(x).Name & "</th> <td><select><option Value='" & rs.Fields(x).Value &
"'>" & rs.Fields(x).Value & "</option></select></td></tr>""")")
                        Case "Div"
                txtstream.WriteLine          ("document.WriteLn(""""<tr><th>"          &
rs.Fields(x).Name      &      "</th><td><div>"      &      rs.Fields(x).Value      &
"</div></td></tr>""")")
                        Case "Listbox"
                txtstream.WriteLine          ("document.WriteLn(""""<tr><th>"          &
rs.Fields(x).Name   &   "</th><td><select  multiple=true><option  Value  ='"   &
rs.Fields(x).Value & "'>" & rs.Fields(x).Value & "</option></select></td></tr>""")")
                        Case "Span"
                txtstream.WriteLine          ("document.WriteLn(""""<tr><th>"          &
rs.Fields(x).Name      &      "</th><td><span>"      &      rs.Fields(x).Value      &
"</span></td></tr>""")")
                        Case "Textbox"
                txtstream.WriteLine          ("document.WriteLn(""""<tr><th>"          &
rs.Fields(x).Name & "</th><td><input type=text Value='" & rs.Fields(x).Value &
"'></input></td></tr>""")")
                        Case "Textarea"
```

```vb
                txtstream.WriteLine        ("document.WriteLn(""<tr><th>"        &
rs.Fields(x).Name       &       "</th><td><textarea>"        &       rs.Fields(x).Value        &
"</textarea></td></tr>"")")

            End Select

        Next

        Case "Multi-Line Vertical"

            Select Case TableType

                Case "Table"

                    txtstream.WriteLine    ("document.WriteLn(""<table    Border='1'
cellpadding='1' cellspacing='1'>"")")

                Case "Report"

                    txtstream.WriteLine    ("document.WriteLn(""<table    Border='0'
cellpadding='1' cellspacing='1'>"")")

            End Select


            For x = 0 To rs.Fields.Count - 1

                txtstream.WriteLine        ("document.WriteLn(""<tr><th>"        &
rs.Fields(x).Name & "</th>"")")

            rs.MoveFirst

            Do While rs.EOF = False

                Select Case ControlType

                    Case "None"
```

```vb
                    txtstream.WriteLine            ("document.WriteLn(""<td>" &
rs.Fields(x).Value & "</td>"")")
                        Case "Button"
                    txtstream.WriteLine ("document.WriteLn(""<td><input type=button
Value='" & rs.Fields(x).Value & "'></input></td>"")")
                        Case "Combobox"
                    txtstream.WriteLine            ("document.WriteLn(""<td><select><option
Value='"    &    rs.Fields(x).Value    &    "'>"    &    rs.Fields(x).Value    &
"</option></select></td>"")")
                        Case "Div"
                    txtstream.WriteLine            ("document.WriteLn(""<td><div>" &
rs.Fields(x).Value & "</div></td>"")")
                        Case "Listbox"
                    txtstream.WriteLine                    ("document.WriteLn(""<td><select
multiple=true><option Value ='" & rs.Fields(x).Value & "'>" & rs.Fields(x).Value &
"</option></select></td>"")")
                        Case "Span"
                    txtstream.WriteLine            ("document.WriteLn(""<td><span>" &
rs.Fields(x).Value & "</span></td>"")")
                        Case "Textbox"
                    txtstream.WriteLine ("document.WriteLn(""<td><input type=text
Value='" & rs.Fields(x).Value & "'></input></td>"")")
                        Case "Textarea"
                    txtstream.WriteLine            ("document.WriteLn(""<td><textarea>" &
rs.Fields(x).Value & "</textarea></td>"")")

                End Select

                rs.MoveNext

            Loop

            txtstream.WriteLine ("document.WriteLn(""</tr>"")")

        Next


    End Select
```

```vbnet
        End If

        txtstream.WriteLine ("document.WriteLn("""</table>""")")
        txtstream.WriteLine (Chr(60) & "/script>")
        txtstream.WriteLine ("</body>")
        txtstream.WriteLine ("</html>")
        txtstream.Close


        tempstr = ""
        Set txtstream = fso.OpenTextFile(ws.CurrentDirectory & "\" & Tablename &
".html", 1, True, -2)
        Do While txtstream.AtEndOfStream = False
            tempstr = tempstr & txtstream.ReadLine()
            tempstr = tempstr & vbCrLf
        Loop
        txtstream.Close
        textarea1.innerText = tempstr

    End Sub

    Sub Do_Cloaked()


        Select Case EngineConfiguration


            Case "cncmdrs"


                Set cn = CreateObject("ADODB.Connection")
                Set cmd = CreateObject("ADODB.Command")
                Set rs = CreateObject("ADODB.Recordset")


                cn.ConnectionString = "Provider=" & Provider & ";Data Source=" &
fName.Value & ";"
                Call cn.Open()

                cmd.ActiveConnection = cn
```

```
        cmd.CommandType = 8
        cmd.CommandText = strQuery
        Call cmd.Execute()

        rs.CursorLocation = 3
        rs.LockType = 3
        Call rs.Open(cmd)


    Case "cnrs"

        Set cn = CreateObject("ADODB.Connection")
        Set rs = CreateObject("ADODB.Recordset")

        cn.ConnectionString = "Provider=" & Provider & ";Data Source=" &
fName.Value & ";"
        Call cn.Open()

        rs.ActiveConnection = cn
        rs.CursorLocation = 3
        rs.LockType = 3
        rs.Source = strQuery
        Call rs.Open()

    Case "cmdrs"

        Set cmd = CreateObject("ADODB.Command")
        Set rs = CreateObject("ADODB.Recordset")

        cmd.ActiveConnection = "Provider=" & Provider & ";Data Source=" &
fName.Value & ";"
        cmd.CommandType = 8
        cmd.CommandText = strQuery
        Call cmd.Execute()

        rs.CursorLocation = 3
        rs.LockType = 3
        Call rs.Open(cmd)

    Case "rs"
```

```vbscript
        Set rs = CreateObject("ADODB.Recordset")
        rs.ActiveConnection = "Provider=" & Provider & ";Data Source=" &
fName.Value & ";"
        rs.LockType = 3
        rs.Cursorlocation = 3
        rs.Source = strQuery
        Call rs.Open()

    End Select


    Set ws = CreateObject("WScript.Shell")
    Set fso = CreateObject("Scripting.FileSystemObject")

    Set txtstream = fso.OpenTextFile(ws.CurrentDirectory & "\" & Tablename &
".html", 2, True, -2)
        txtstream.WriteLine ("<html>")
        txtstream.WriteLine ("<head>")
        txtstream.WriteLine ("<title>" & Tablename & "</title>")

    Add_The_StyleSheet

        txtstream.WriteLine ("</head>")
        txtstream.WriteLine ("<body>")
        txtstream.WriteLine ("<script language='vbscript'>")
        txtstream.WriteLine ("")
        txtstream.WriteLine ("dim mystr")
        txtstream.WriteLine ("")
        txtstream.WriteLine ("Sub Window_OnLoad()")
        txtstream.WriteLine ("")

    If StyleSheet = "InLine" Then


        Select Case Orientation


            Case "Single-Line Horizontal"
```

```vba
Select Case TableType

    Case "Table"

        txtstream.WriteLine ("mystr = mystr & ""<table Border='1'
cellpadding='1' cellspacing='1' datasrc=#rs>"" & vbcrlf")

    Case "Report"

        txtstream.WriteLine ("mystr = mystr & ""<table Border='0'
cellpadding='1' cellspacing='1' datasrc=#rs>"" & vbcrlf")

End Select


txtstream.WriteLine ("mystr = mystr & ""<tr>"" & vbcrlf")
For x = 0 To rs.Fields.Count - 1

        txtstream.WriteLine ("mystr = mystr & ""<th style='font-
family:Calibri, Sans-Serif;font-size: 12px;color:darkred;'>" & rs.Fields(x).Name &
"</th>"" & vbcrlf")

Next
txtstream.WriteLine ("mystr = mystr & ""</tr>"" & vbcrlf")
txtstream.WriteLine ("mystr = mystr & ""<tr>"" & vbcrlf")
For x = 0 To rs.Fields.Count - 1


    Select Case ControlType

        Case "None"
        txtstream.WriteLine ("mystr = mystr & ""<td style='font-
family:Calibri, Sans-Serif;font-size: 12px;color:navy;'>" & rs.Fields(x).Value &
"</td>"" & vbcrlf")
        Case "Button"
        txtstream.WriteLine ("mystr = mystr & ""<td style='font-
family:Calibri, Sans-Serif;font-size: 12px;color:navy;'><input type=button Value='"
& rs.Fields(x).Value & "'></input></td>"" & vbcrlf")
        Case "Combobox"
```

```
            txtstream.WriteLine ("mystr = mystr & ""<td style='font-
family:Calibri, Sans-Serif;font-size: 12px;color:navy;'><select><option Value='" &
rs.Fields(x).Value & "'>" & rs.Fields(x).Value & "</option></select></td>""" &
vbcrlf")
        Case "Div"
            txtstream.WriteLine ("mystr = mystr & ""<td style='font-
family:Calibri, Sans-Serif;font-size: 12px;color:navy;'><div>" & rs.Fields(x).Value &
"</div></td>""" & vbcrlf")
        Case "Listbox"
            txtstream.WriteLine ("mystr = mystr & ""<td style='font-
family:Calibri,        Sans-Serif;font-size:          12px;color:navy;'><select
multiple=true><option Value ='" & rs.Fields(x).Value & "'>" & rs.Fields(x).Value &
"</option></select></td>""" & vbcrlf")
        Case "Span"
            txtstream.WriteLine ("mystr = mystr & ""<td style='font-
family:Calibri, Sans-Serif;font-size: 12px;color:navy;'><span>" & rs.Fields(x).Value
& "</span></td>""" & vbcrlf")
        Case "Textbox"
            txtstream.WriteLine ("mystr = mystr & ""<td style='font-
family:Calibri, Sans-Serif;font-size: 12px;color:navy;'><input type=text Value='" &
rs.Fields(x).Value & "'></input></td>""" & vbcrlf")
        Case "Textarea"
            txtstream.WriteLine ("mystr = mystr & ""<td style='font-
family:Calibri,      Sans-Serif;font-size:      12px;color:navy;'><textarea>"      &
rs.Fields(x).Value & "</textarea></td>""" & vbcrlf")


        End Select



    Next

        txtstream.WriteLine ("mystr = mystr & ""</tr>""" & vbcrlf")


    Case "Multi-Line Horizontal"


    Select Case TableType
```

```vb
                Case "Table"

                        txtstream.WriteLine ("mystr = mystr & ""<table Border='1'
cellpadding='1' cellspacing='1'>"" & vbcrlf")

                Case "Report"

                        txtstream.WriteLine ("mystr = mystr & ""<table Border='0'
cellpadding='1' cellspacing='1'>"" & vbcrlf")

        End Select

        txtstream.WriteLine ("mystr = mystr & ""<tr>"" & vbcrlf")
        For x = 0 To rs.Fields.Count - 1

                txtstream.WriteLine ("mystr = mystr & ""<th style='font-
family:Calibri, Sans-Serif;font-size: 12px;color:darkred;'>" & rs.Fields(x).Name &
"</th>"" & vbcrlf")

        Next
        txtstream.WriteLine ("mystr = mystr & ""</tr>"" & vbcrlf")
        Do While rs.EOF = False

                txtstream.WriteLine ("mystr = mystr & ""<tr>"" & vbcrlf")
                For x = 0 To rs.Fields.Count - 1

                Select Case ControlType

                        Case "None"
                txtstream.WriteLine ("mystr = mystr & ""<td style='font-
family:Calibri, Sans-Serif;font-size: 12px;color:navy;'>" & rs.Fields(x).Value &
"</td>"" & vbcrlf")
                        Case "Button"
                txtstream.WriteLine ("mystr = mystr & ""<td style='font-
family:Calibri, Sans-Serif;font-size: 12px;color:navy;'><input type=button Value=""
& rs.Fields(x).Value & "'></input></td>"" & vbcrlf")
                        Case "Combobox"
                txtstream.WriteLine ("mystr = mystr & ""<td style='font-
family:Calibri, Sans-Serif;font-size: 12px;color:navy;'><select><option Value='" &
```

```vb
rs.Fields(x).Value & "'>" & rs.Fields(x).Value & "</option></select></td>""" & vbcrlf")
            Case "Div"
                txtstream.WriteLine ("mystr = mystr & ""<td style='font-family:Calibri, Sans-Serif;font-size: 12px;color:navy;'><div>" & rs.Fields(x).Value & "</div></td>""" & vbcrlf")
            Case "Listbox"
                txtstream.WriteLine ("mystr = mystr & ""<td style='font-family:Calibri,         Sans-Serif;font-size:        12px;color:navy;'><select multiple=true><option Value ='" & rs.Fields(x).Value & "'>" & rs.Fields(x).Value & "</option></select></td>""" & vbcrlf")
            Case "Span"
                txtstream.WriteLine ("mystr = mystr & ""<td style='font-family:Calibri, Sans-Serif;font-size: 12px;color:navy;'><span>" & rs.Fields(x).Value & "</span></td>""" & vbcrlf")
            Case "Textbox"
                txtstream.WriteLine ("mystr = mystr & ""<td style='font-family:Calibri, Sans-Serif;font-size: 12px;color:navy;'><input type=text Value='" & rs.Fields(x).Value & "'></input></td>""" & vbcrlf")
            Case "Textarea"
                txtstream.WriteLine ("mystr = mystr & ""<td style='font-family:Calibri,     Sans-Serif;font-size:     12px;color:navy;'><textarea>"     & rs.Fields(x).Value & "</textarea></td>""" & vbcrlf")

        End Select


    Next
    txtstream.WriteLine ("mystr = mystr & ""</tr>""" & vbcrlf")
    rs.MoveNext
    Loop



Case "Single-Line Vertical"


    Select Case TableType


    Case "Table"
```

```vb
            txtstream.WriteLine ("mystr = mystr & ""<table Border='1'
cellpadding='1' cellspacing='1'>""" & vbcrlf")

        Case "Report"

            txtstream.WriteLine ("mystr = mystr & ""<table Border='0'
cellpadding='1' cellspacing='1'>""" & vbcrlf")

        End Select

        For x = 0 To rs.Fields.Count - 1

            Select Case ControlType

                Case "None"
                txtstream.WriteLine ("mystr = mystr & ""<tr><th style='font-
family:Calibri, Sans-Serif;font-size: 12px;color:darkred;'>" & rs.Fields(x).Name &
"</th><td style='font-family:Calibri, Sans-Serif;font-size: 12px;color:navy;'>" &
rs.Fields(x).Value & "</td></tr>""" & vbcrlf")
                Case "Button"
                txtstream.WriteLine ("mystr = mystr & ""<tr><th style='font-
family:Calibri, Sans-Serif;font-size: 12px;color:darkred;'>" & rs.Fields(x).Name &
"</th><td style='font-family:Calibri, Sans-Serif;font-size: 12px;color:navy;'><input
type=button Value='" & rs.Fields(x).Value & "'></input></td></tr>""" & vbcrlf")
                Case "Combobox"
                txtstream.WriteLine ("mystr = mystr & ""<tr><th style='font-
family:Calibri, Sans-Serif;font-size: 12px;color:darkred;'>" & rs.Fields(x).Name &
"</th>          <td          style='font-family:Calibri,          Sans-Serif;font-size:
12px;color:navy;'><select><option Value='" & rs.Fields(x).Value & "'>" &
rs.Fields(x).Value & "</option></select></td></tr>""" & vbcrlf")
                Case "Div"
                txtstream.WriteLine ("mystr = mystr & ""<tr><th style='font-
family:Calibri, Sans-Serif;font-size: 12px;color:darkred;'>" & rs.Fields(x).Name &
"</th><td style='font-family:Calibri, Sans-Serif;font-size: 12px;color:navy;'><div>"
& rs.Fields(x).Value & "</div></td></tr>""" & vbcrlf")
                Case "Listbox"
                txtstream.WriteLine ("mystr = mystr & ""<tr><th style='font-
family:Calibri, Sans-Serif;font-size: 12px;color:darkred;'>" & rs.Fields(x).Name &
"</th><td style='font-family:Calibri, Sans-Serif;font-size: 12px;color:navy;'><select
```

```
multiple=true><option Value ='" & rs.Fields(x).Value & "'>" & rs.Fields(x).Value &
"</option></select></td></tr>"" & vbcrlf")
                Case "Span"
            txtstream.WriteLine ("mystr = mystr & ""<tr><th style='font-
family:Calibri, Sans-Serif;font-size: 12px;color:darkred;'>" & rs.Fields(x).Name &
"</th><td        style='font-family:Calibri,        Sans-Serif;font-size:
12px;color:navy;'><span>" & rs.Fields(x).Value & "</span></td></tr>"" & vbcrlf")
                Case "Textbox"
            txtstream.WriteLine ("mystr = mystr & ""<tr><th style='font-
family:Calibri, Sans-Serif;font-size: 12px;color:darkred;'>" & rs.Fields(x).Name &
"</th><td style='font-family:Calibri, Sans-Serif;font-size: 12px;color:navy;'><input
type=text Value='" & rs.Fields(x).Value & "'></input></td></tr>"" & vbcrlf")
                Case "Textarea"
            txtstream.WriteLine ("mystr = mystr & ""<tr><th style='font-
family:Calibri, Sans-Serif;font-size: 12px;color:darkred;'>" & rs.Fields(x).Name &
"</th><td        style='font-family:Calibri,        Sans-Serif;font-size:
12px;color:navy;'><textarea>" & rs.Fields(x).Value & "</textarea></td></tr>"" &
vbcrlf")


            End Select

        Next


    Case "Multi-Line Vertical"


        Select Case TableType

            Case "Table"

                txtstream.WriteLine ("mystr = mystr & ""<table Border='1'
cellpadding='1' cellspacing='1'>"" & vbcrlf")

            Case "Report"

                txtstream.WriteLine ("mystr = mystr & ""<table Border='0'
cellpadding='1' cellspacing='1'>"" & vbcrlf")

        End Select
```

```
For x = 0 To rs.Fields.Count - 1

        txtstream.WriteLine ("mystr = mystr & ""<tr><th style='font-
family:Calibri, Sans-Serif;font-size: 12px;color:darkred;'>" & rs.Fields(x).Name &
"</th>""" & vbcrlf")

        rs.MoveFirst

        Do While rs.EOF = False


            Select Case ControlType

                Case "None"
                txtstream.WriteLine ("mystr = mystr & ""<td style='font-
family:Calibri, Sans-Serif;font-size: 12px;color:navy;'>" & rs.Fields(x).Value &
"</td>""" & vbcrlf")
                Case "Button"
                txtstream.WriteLine ("mystr = mystr & ""<td style='font-
family:Calibri, Sans-Serif;font-size: 12px;color:navy;'><input type=button Value='"
& rs.Fields(x).Value & "'></input></td>""" & vbcrlf")
                Case "Combobox"
                txtstream.WriteLine ("mystr = mystr & ""<td style='font-
family:Calibri, Sans-Serif;font-size: 12px;color:navy;'><select><option Value='" &
rs.Fields(x).Value & "'>" & rs.Fields(x).Value & "</option></select></td>""" &
vbcrlf")
                Case "Div"
                txtstream.WriteLine ("mystr = mystr & ""<td style='font-
family:Calibri, Sans-Serif;font-size: 12px;color:navy;'><div>" & rs.Fields(x).Value &
"</div></td>""" & vbcrlf")
                Case "Listbox"
                txtstream.WriteLine ("mystr = mystr & ""<td style='font-
family:Calibri,        Sans-Serif;font-size:        12px;color:navy;'><select
multiple=true><option Value ='" & rs.Fields(x).Value & "'>" & rs.Fields(x).Value &
"</option></select></td>""" & vbcrlf")
                Case "Span"
```

```vbnet
            txtstream.WriteLine ("mystr  =  mystr  &  """<td  style='font-
family:Calibri, Sans-Serif;font-size: 12px;color:navy;'><span>" & rs.Fields(x).Value
& "</span></td>""" & vbcrlf")
                Case "Textbox"
            txtstream.WriteLine ("mystr  =  mystr  &  """<td  style='font-
family:Calibri, Sans-Serif;font-size: 12px;color:navy;'><input type=text Value='" &
rs.Fields(x).Value & "'></input></td>""" & vbcrlf")
                Case "Textarea"
            txtstream.WriteLine ("mystr  =  mystr  &  """<td  style='font-
family:Calibri,   Sans-Serif;font-size:   12px;color:navy;'><textarea>"   &
rs.Fields(x).Value & "</textarea></td>""" & vbcrlf")

            End Select

            rs.MoveNext

        Loop

        txtstream.WriteLine ("mystr = mystr & """</tr>""" & vbcrlf")

    Next


    End Select



Else


    Select Case Orientation


        Case "Single-Line Horizontal"

        Select Case TableType

            Case "Table"
```

```vbnet
                    txtstream.WriteLine ("mystr = mystr & """<table Border='1'
cellpadding='1' cellspacing='1' datasrc=#rs>""" & vbcrlf")

            Case "Report"

                    txtstream.WriteLine ("mystr = mystr & """<table Border='0'
cellpadding='1' cellspacing='1' datasrc=#rs>""" & vbcrlf")

            End Select


            txtstream.WriteLine ("mystr = mystr & """<tr>""" & vbcrlf")
            For x = 0 To rs.Fields.Count - 1

                    txtstream.WriteLine ("mystr  =  mystr  &  """<th>"  &
rs.Fields(x).Name & "</th>""" & vbcrlf")

            Next
            txtstream.WriteLine ("mystr = mystr & """</tr>""" & vbcrlf")
            txtstream.WriteLine ("mystr = mystr & """<tr>""" & vbcrlf")
            For x = 0 To rs.Fields.Count - 1


            Select Case ControlType

                Case "None"
            txtstream.WriteLine ("mystr = mystr & """<td>" & rs.Fields(x).Value &
"</td>""" & vbcrlf")
                Case "Button"
            txtstream.WriteLine ("mystr = mystr & """<td><input type=button
Value='" & rs.Fields(x).Value & "'></input></td>""" & vbcrlf")
                Case "Combobox"
            txtstream.WriteLine ("mystr  =  mystr  &  """<td><select><option
Value='"   &   rs.Fields(x).Value   &   "'>"   &   rs.Fields(x).Value   &
"</option></select></td>""" & vbcrlf")
                Case "Div"
            txtstream.WriteLine ("mystr  =  mystr  &  """<td><div>"  &
rs.Fields(x).Value & "</div></td>""" & vbcrlf")
                Case "Listbox"
```

```vb
                txtstream.WriteLine    ("mystr    =    mystr    &    """<td><select
multiple=true><option Value ='" & rs.Fields(x).Value & "'>" & rs.Fields(x).Value &
"</option></select></td>""" & vbcrlf")
                Case "Span"
                txtstream.WriteLine    ("mystr    =    mystr    &    """<td><span>"    &
rs.Fields(x).Value & "</span></td>""" & vbcrlf")
                Case "Textbox"
                txtstream.WriteLine ("mystr = mystr & """<td><input type=text
Value='" & rs.Fields(x).Value & "'></input></td>""" & vbcrlf")
                Case "Textarea"
                txtstream.WriteLine    ("mystr    =    mystr    &    """<td><textarea>"    &
rs.Fields(x).Value & "</textarea></td>""" & vbcrlf")

            End Select


            Next

            txtstream.WriteLine ("mystr = mystr & """</tr>""" & vbcrlf")


        Case "Multi-Line Horizontal"


            Select Case TableType

                Case "Table"

                    txtstream.WriteLine ("mystr = mystr & """<table Border='1'
cellpadding='1' cellspacing='1'>""" & vbcrlf")

                Case "Report"

                    txtstream.WriteLine ("mystr = mystr & """<table Border='0'
cellpadding='1' cellspacing='1'>""" & vbcrlf")

            End Select

            txtstream.WriteLine ("mystr = mystr & """<tr>""" & vbcrlf")
```

```vb
                For x = 0 To rs.Fields.Count - 1

                    txtstream.WriteLine     ("mystr     =     mystr     &     """<th>"     &
rs.Fields(x).Name & "</th>""" & vbcrlf)

                Next
                txtstream.WriteLine ("mystr = mystr & """</tr>""" & vbcrlf)
                Do While rs.EOF = False

                    txtstream.WriteLine ("mystr = mystr & """<tr>""" & vbcrlf)
                    For x = 0 To rs.Fields.Count - 1

                    Select Case ControlType

                        Case "None"
                        txtstream.WriteLine ("mystr = mystr & """<td>" & rs.Fields(x).Value
& "</td>""" & vbcrlf)
                        Case "Button"
                        txtstream.WriteLine ("mystr = mystr & """<td><input type=button
Value='" & rs.Fields(x).Value & "'></input></td>""" & vbcrlf)
                        Case "Combobox"
                        txtstream.WriteLine     ("mystr     =     mystr     &     """<td><select><option
Value='"     &     rs.Fields(x).Value     &     "'>"     &     rs.Fields(x).Value     &
"</option></select></td>""" & vbcrlf)
                        Case "Div"
                        txtstream.WriteLine     ("mystr     =     mystr     &     """<td><div>"     &
rs.Fields(x).Value & "</div></td>""" & vbcrlf)
                        Case "Listbox"
                        txtstream.WriteLine     ("mystr     =     mystr     &     """<td><select
multiple=true><option Value ='" & rs.Fields(x).Value & "'>" & rs.Fields(x).Value &
"</option></select></td>""" & vbcrlf)
                        Case "Span"
                        txtstream.WriteLine     ("mystr     =     mystr     &     """<td><span>"     &
rs.Fields(x).Value & "</span></td>""" & vbcrlf)
                        Case "Textbox"
                        txtstream.WriteLine ("mystr = mystr & """<td><input type=text
Value='" & rs.Fields(x).Value & "'></input></td>""" & vbcrlf)
                        Case "Textarea"
                        txtstream.WriteLine     ("mystr     =     mystr     &     """<td><textarea>"     &
rs.Fields(x).Value & "</textarea></td>""" & vbcrlf)
```

```
            End Select


        Next
        txtstream.WriteLine ("mystr = mystr & """"</tr>"""" & vbcrlf")
        rs.MoveNext
    Loop



    Case "Single-Line Vertical"


        Select Case TableType

            Case "Table"

                txtstream.WriteLine ("mystr = mystr & """"<table Border='1'
cellpadding='1' cellspacing='1'>"""" & vbcrlf")

            Case "Report"

                txtstream.WriteLine ("mystr = mystr & """"<table Border='0'
cellpadding='1' cellspacing='1'>"""" & vbcrlf")

        End Select

        For x = 0 To rs.Fields.Count - 1

            Select Case ControlType

                Case "None"
                txtstream.WriteLine    ("mystr =    mystr   &   """"<tr><th>"   &
rs.Fields(x).Name & "</th><td>" & rs.Fields(x).Value & "</td></tr>"""" & vbcrlf")
                Case "Button"
                txtstream.WriteLine    ("mystr =    mystr   &   """"<tr><th>"   &
rs.Fields(x).Name & "</th><td><input type=button Value='" & rs.Fields(x).Value &
"'></input></td></tr>"""" & vbcrlf")
                Case "Combobox"
```

```
                    txtstream.WriteLine    ("mystr  =  mystr  &  ""<tr><th>"  &
rs.Fields(x).Name & "</th> <td><select><option Value='" & rs.Fields(x).Value &
"'>" & rs.Fields(x).Value & "</option></select></td></tr>"" & vbcrlf")
                        Case "Div"
                    txtstream.WriteLine    ("mystr  =  mystr  &  ""<tr><th>"  &
rs.Fields(x).Name & "</th><td><div>" & rs.Fields(x).Value & "</div></td></tr>"" &
vbcrlf")
                        Case "Listbox"
                    txtstream.WriteLine    ("mystr  =  mystr  &  ""<tr><th>"  &
rs.Fields(x).Name  &  "</th><td><select  multiple=true><option  Value ='"  &
rs.Fields(x).Value & "'>" & rs.Fields(x).Value & "</option></select></td></tr>"" &
vbcrlf")
                        Case "Span"
                    txtstream.WriteLine    ("mystr  =  mystr  &  ""<tr><th>"  &
rs.Fields(x).Name    &    "</th><td><span>"    &    rs.Fields(x).Value    &
"</span></td></tr>"" & vbcrlf")
                        Case "Textbox"
                    txtstream.WriteLine    ("mystr  =  mystr  &  ""<tr><th>"  &
rs.Fields(x).Name & "</th><td><input type=text Value='" & rs.Fields(x).Value &
"'></input></td></tr>"" & vbcrlf")
                        Case "Textarea"
                    txtstream.WriteLine    ("mystr  =  mystr  &  ""<tr><th>"  &
rs.Fields(x).Name    &    "</th><td><textarea>"    &    rs.Fields(x).Value    &
"</textarea></td></tr>"" & vbcrlf")


                End Select

            Next



            Case "Multi-Line Vertical"


            Select Case TableType

            Case "Table"


                    txtstream.WriteLine ("mystr = mystr & ""<table Border='1'
cellpadding='1' cellspacing='1'>"" & vbcrlf")
```

```
Case "Report"

        txtstream.WriteLine ("mystr = mystr & ""<table Border='0'
cellpadding='1' cellspacing='1'>"" & vbcrlf")

    End Select


    For x = 0 To rs.Fields.Count - 1

        txtstream.WriteLine ("mystr  =  mystr  &  ""<tr><th>"  &
rs.Fields(x).Name & "</th>"" & vbcrlf")

    rs.MoveFirst

    Do While rs.EOF = False


        Select Case ControlType

            Case "None"
            txtstream.WriteLine ("mystr = mystr & ""<td>" & rs.Fields(x).Value
& "</td>"" & vbcrlf")
            Case "Button"
            txtstream.WriteLine ("mystr = mystr & ""<td><input type=button
Value='" & rs.Fields(x).Value & "'></input></td>"" & vbcrlf")
            Case "Combobox"
            txtstream.WriteLine ("mystr  =  mystr  &  ""<td><select><option
Value='"    &    rs.Fields(x).Value    &    "'>"    &    rs.Fields(x).Value    &
"</option></select></td>"" & vbcrlf")
            Case "Div"
            txtstream.WriteLine  ("mystr  =  mystr  &  ""<td><div>"  &
rs.Fields(x).Value & "</div></td>"" & vbcrlf")
            Case "Listbox"
            txtstream.WriteLine  ("mystr  =  mystr  &  ""<td><select
multiple=true><option Value ='" & rs.Fields(x).Value & "'>" & rs.Fields(x).Value &
"</option></select></td>"" & vbcrlf")
            Case "Span"
            txtstream.WriteLine  ("mystr  =  mystr  &  ""<td><span>"  &
rs.Fields(x).Value & "</span></td>"" & vbcrlf")
```

```
                Case "Textbox"
            txtstream.WriteLine ("mystr = mystr & ""<td><input type=text
Value='" & rs.Fields(x).Value & "'></input></td>"" & vbcrlf")
                Case "Textarea"
            txtstream.WriteLine ("mystr = mystr & ""<td><textarea>" &
rs.Fields(x).Value & "</textarea></td>"" & vbcrlf")

        End Select

        rs.MoveNext

    Loop

        txtstream.WriteLine ("mystr = mystr & ""</tr>"" & vbcrlf")

    Next


    End Select


End If

    txtstream.WriteLine ("mystr = mystr & ""</table>"" & vbcrlf")
    txtstream.WriteLine ("document.WriteLn(mystr)")
    txtstream.WriteLine ("")
    txtstream.WriteLine ("End Sub")
    txtstream.WriteLine ("")
    txtstream.WriteLine (Chr(60) & "/script>")
    txtstream.WriteLine ("</body>")
    txtstream.WriteLine ("</html>")
    txtstream.Close


    tempstr = ""
    Set txtstream = fso.OpenTextFile(ws.CurrentDirectory & "\" & Tablename &
".html", 1, True, -2)
    Do While txtstream.AtEndOfStream = False
        tempstr = tempstr & txtstream.ReadLine()
```

```vb
            tempstr = tempstr & vbCrLf
        Loop
        txtstream.Close
        textarea1.innerText = tempstr

End Sub

Sub Do_Bound()

    Select Case EngineConfiguration


        Case "cncmdrs"


            Set cn = CreateObject("ADODB.Connection")
            Set cmd = CreateObject("ADODB.Command")
            Set rs = CreateObject("ADODB.Recordset")


            cn.ConnectionString = "Provider=" & provider & ";Data Source=" &
fName.Value & ";"
            Call cn.Open()

            cmd.ActiveConnection = cn
            cmd.CommandType = 8
            cmd.CommandText = strQuery
            Call cmd.Execute()

            rs.CursorLocation = 3
            rs.LockType = 3
            Call rs.Open(cmd)


        Case "cnrs"

            Set cn = CreateObject("ADODB.Connection")
            Set rs = CreateObject("ADODB.Recordset")
```

```vbscript
            cn.ConnectionString = "Provider=" & Provider & ";Data Source=" &
fName.Value & ";"
            Call cn.Open()

            rs.ActiveConnection = cn
            rs.CursorLocation = 3
            rs.LockType = 3
            rs.Source = strQuery
            Call rs.Open()

        Case "cmdrs"

            Set cmd = CreateObject("ADODB.Command")
            Set rs = CreateObject("ADODB.Recordset")

            cmd.ActiveConnection = "Provider=" & Provider & ";Data Source=" &
fName.Value & ";"
            cmd.CommandType = 8
            cmd.CommandText = strQuery
            Call cmd.Execute()

            rs.CursorLocation = 3
            rs.LockType = 3
            Call rs.Open(cmd)

        Case "rs"

            Set rs = CreateObject("ADODB.Recordset")
            rs.ActiveConnection = "Provider=" & Provider & ";Data Source=" &
fName.Value & ";"
            rs.LockType = 3
            rs.Cursorlocation = 3
            rs.Source = strQuery
            Call rs.Open()

    End Select

        Set ws = CreateObject("WScript.Shell")
        Set fso = CreateObject("Scripting.FileSystemObject")
```

```
        Set txtstream = fso.OpenTextFile(ws.CurrentDirectory & "\" & Tablename &
".html", 2, True, -2)
        txtstream.WriteLine ("<html>")
        txtstream.WriteLine ("<head>")
        txtstream.WriteLine ("<title>" & Tablename & "</title>")


    Add_The_StyleSheet



    Select Case HTMLEngineConfiguration



        Case "cncmdrs"


            txtstream.WriteLine ("<object id=""cmd"" CLASSID=""clsid:00000507-
0000-0010-8000-00AA006D2EA4"" height=""0"" width=""0""></object>")
            txtstream.WriteLine ("<object id=""cn"" CLASSID=""clsid:00000514-
0000-0010-8000-00AA006D2EA4"" height=""0"" width=""0""></object>")
            txtstream.WriteLine ("<object id=""rs"" CLASSID=""clsid:00000535-
0000-0010-8000-00AA006D2EA4"" height=""0"" width=""0""></object>")
        txtstream.WriteLine ("</head>")
        txtstream.WriteLine ("<body>")
        txtstream.WriteLine ("<script language='vbscript'>")
        txtstream.WriteLine ("")
        txtstream.WriteLine ("cn.ConnectionString = ""Provider=" & Provider &
";Data Source=" & fName.Value & ";"" ")
        txtstream.WriteLine ("Call cn.Open()")
        txtstream.WriteLine ("")
        txtstream.WriteLine ("cmd.ActiveConnection = cn")
        txtstream.WriteLine ("cmd.CommandType = 8")
        txtstream.WriteLine ("cmd.CommandText = """" & strQuery & """" ")
        txtstream.WriteLine ("Call cmd.Execute()")
        txtstream.WriteLine ("")
        txtstream.WriteLine ("rs.CursorLocation = 3")
        txtstream.WriteLine ("rs.LockType = 3")
        txtstream.WriteLine ("Call rs.Open(cmd)")
        txtstream.WriteLine ("")
        txtstream.WriteLine (Chr(60) & "/script>")
```

```vbscript
        Case "cnrs"

            txtstream.WriteLine ("<object id=""""cn"""" CLASSID=""""clsid:00000514-0000-
0010-8000-00AA006D2EA4"""" height=""""0"""" width=""""0""""></object>")
            txtstream.WriteLine ("<object id=""""rs"""" CLASSID=""""clsid:00000535-0000-
0010-8000-00AA006D2EA4"""" height=""""0"""" width=""""0""""></object>")
            txtstream.WriteLine ("</head>")
            txtstream.WriteLine ("<body>")
            txtstream.WriteLine ("<script language='vbscript'>")
            txtstream.WriteLine ("")
            txtstream.WriteLine ("cn.ConnectionString = """"Provider=" & Provider &
";Data Source=" & fName.Value & ";"""" ")
            txtstream.WriteLine ("Call cn.Open()")
            txtstream.WriteLine ("")
            txtstream.WriteLine ("rs.ActiveConnection = cn")
            txtstream.WriteLine ("rs.CursorLocation = 3")
            txtstream.WriteLine ("rs.LockType = 3")
            txtstream.WriteLine ("rs.Source = """""" & strQuery & """""" ")
            txtstream.WriteLine ("Call rs.Open()")
            txtstream.WriteLine ("")
            txtstream.WriteLine (Chr(60) & "/script>")


        Case "cmdrs"

            txtstream.WriteLine ("<object id=""""cmd"""" CLASSID=""""clsid:00000507-
0000-0010-8000-00AA006D2EA4"""" height=""""0"""" width=""""0""""></object>")
            txtstream.WriteLine ("<object id=""""rs"""" CLASSID=""""clsid:00000535-
0000-0010-8000-00AA006D2EA4"""" height=""""0"""" width=""""0""""></object>")
            txtstream.WriteLine ("</head>")
            txtstream.WriteLine ("<body>")
            txtstream.WriteLine ("<script language='vbscript'>")
            txtstream.WriteLine ("")
            txtstream.WriteLine ("cmd.ActiveConnection = """"Provider=" & Provider &
";Data Source=" & fName.Value & ";"""" ")
            txtstream.WriteLine ("cmd.CommandType = 8")
            txtstream.WriteLine ("cmd.CommandText = """""" & strQuery & """""" ")
            txtstream.WriteLine ("Call cmd.Execute()")
```

```
        txtstream.WriteLine ("")
        txtstream.WriteLine ("rs.CursorLocation = 3")
        txtstream.WriteLine ("rs.LockType = 3")
        txtstream.WriteLine ("Call rs.Open(cmd)")
        txtstream.WriteLine ("")
        txtstream.WriteLine (Chr(60) & "/script>")

    Case "rs"



        txtstream.WriteLine ("<object id=""rs"" CLASSID=""clsid:00000535-0000-
0010-8000-00AA006D2EA4"" height=""0"" width=""0""></object>")
        txtstream.WriteLine ("</head>")
        txtstream.WriteLine ("<body>")
        txtstream.WriteLine ("<script language='vbscript'>")
        txtstream.WriteLine ("")
        txtstream.WriteLine ("rs.ActiveConnection = ""Provider=" & Provider &
";Data Source=" & fName.Value & ";"" ")
        txtstream.WriteLine ("rs.LockType = 3")
        txtstream.WriteLine ("rs.Cursorlocation = 3")
        txtstream.WriteLine ("rs.Source = """ & strQuery & """ ")
        txtstream.WriteLine ("Call rs.Open()")
        txtstream.WriteLine ("")
        txtstream.WriteLine (Chr(60) & "/script>")

    End Select


    If StyleSheet = "InLine" Then


        Select Case Orientation


            Case "Single-Line Horizontal"

            Select Case TableType

                Case "Table"
```

```
                txtstream.WriteLine    ("<table    Border='1'    cellpadding='1'
cellspacing='1'>")

        Case "Report"

                txtstream.WriteLine    ("<table    Border='0'    cellpadding='1'
cellspacing='1'>")

        End Select


        txtstream.WriteLine ("<tr>")
        For x = 0 To rs.Fields.Count - 1

                txtstream.WriteLine    ("<th    style='font-family:Calibri,    Sans-
Serif;font-size: 12px;color:darkred;'>" & rs.Fields(x).Name & "</th>")

        Next
        txtstream.WriteLine ("</tr>")
        txtstream.WriteLine ("<tr>")
        For x = 0 To rs.Fields.Count - 1

        Select Case ControlType

            Case "Button"
        txtstream.WriteLine ("<td style='font-family:Calibri, Sans-Serif;font-
size:    12px;color:navy;'><input    type=button    datasrc=#rs    datafld='"    &
rs.Fields(x).Name & "'></input></td>")
            Case "Combobox"
        txtstream.WriteLine ("<td style='font-family:Calibri, Sans-Serif;font-
size: 12px;color:navy;'><select datasrc=#rs datafld='" & rs.Fields(x).Name &
"'></select></td>")
            Case "Div"
        txtstream.WriteLine ("<td style='font-family:Calibri, Sans-Serif;font-
size:    12px;color:navy;'><div    datasrc=#rs    datafld='"    &    rs.Fields(x).Name    &
"'></div></td>")
            Case "Listbox"
```

```
                txtstream.WriteLine ("<td style='font-family:Calibri, Sans-Serif;font-
size:   12px;color:navy;'><select    multiple=true    datasrc=#rs    datafld='"    &
rs.Fields(x).Name & "'></option></select></td>")
                Case "Span"
                txtstream.WriteLine ("<td style='font-family:Calibri, Sans-Serif;font-
size:  12px;color:navy;'><span  datasrc=#rs  datafld='"  &  rs.Fields(x).Name  &
"'></span></td>")
                Case "Textbox"
                txtstream.WriteLine ("<td style='font-family:Calibri, Sans-Serif;font-
size: 12px;color:navy;'><input type=text datasrc=#rs datafld='" & rs.Fields(x).Name
& "'></input></td>")
                Case "Textarea"
                txtstream.WriteLine ("<td style='font-family:Calibri, Sans-Serif;font-
size:  12px;color:navy;'><textarea  datasrc=#rs  datafld='"  &  rs.Fields(x).Name  &
"'></textarea></td>")

            End Select

        Next

        txtstream.WriteLine ("</tr>")


    Case "Multi-Line Horizontal"


        Select Case TableType

            Case "Table"

                txtstream.WriteLine      ("<table    Border='1'    cellpadding='1'
cellspacing='1' datasrc=#rs>")

            Case "Report"

                txtstream.WriteLine      ("<table    Border='0'    cellpadding='1'
cellspacing='1' datasrc=#rs>")

        End Select
```

```
txtstream.WriteLine ("<thead><tr>")
For x = 0 To rs.Fields.Count - 1

    txtstream.WriteLine ("<th style='font-family:Calibri, Sans-
Serif;font-size: 12px;color:darkred;'>" & rs.Fields(x).Name & "</th>")

Next
txtstream.WriteLine ("</tr></thead>")
txtstream.WriteLine ("<tbody><tr>")
For x = 0 To rs.Fields.Count - 1

    Select Case ControlType

        Case "Button"
        txtstream.WriteLine ("<td style='font-family:Calibri, Sans-Serif;font-
size:   12px;color:navy;'><input   type=button   datasrc=#rs   datafld='"   &
rs.Fields(x).Name & "'></input></td>")
        Case "Combobox"
        txtstream.WriteLine ("<td style='font-family:Calibri, Sans-Serif;font-
size:  12px;color:navy;'><select datasrc=#rs  datafld='"  & rs.Fields(x).Name  &
"'></select></td>")
        Case "Div"
        txtstream.WriteLine ("<td style='font-family:Calibri, Sans-Serif;font-
size:  12px;color:navy;'><div  datasrc=#rs  datafld='"  &  rs.Fields(x).Name  &
"'></div></td>")
        Case "Listbox"
        txtstream.WriteLine ("<td style='font-family:Calibri, Sans-Serif;font-
size:   12px;color:navy;'><select   multiple=true   datasrc=#rs   datafld='"   &
rs.Fields(x).Name & "'></option></select></td>")
        Case "Span"
        txtstream.WriteLine ("<td style='font-family:Calibri, Sans-Serif;font-
size:  12px;color:navy;'><span datasrc=#rs  datafld='"  & rs.Fields(x).Name  &
"'></span></td>")
        Case "Textbox"
        txtstream.WriteLine ("<td style='font-family:Calibri, Sans-Serif;font-
size: 12px;color:navy;'><input type=text datasrc=#rs datafld='" & rs.Fields(x).Name
& "'></input></td>")
        Case "Textarea"
```

```
            txtstream.WriteLine ("<td style='font-family:Calibri, Sans-Serif;font-
size: 12px;color:navy;'><textarea datasrc=#rs datafld='" & rs.Fields(x).Name &
"'></textarea></td>")

            End Select

         Next

            txtstream.WriteLine ("</tr></tbody>")


         Case "Single-Line Vertical"

            Select Case TableType

               Case "Table"

                  txtstream.WriteLine    ("<table    Border='1'    cellpadding='1'
cellspacing='1'>")

                  Case "Report"

                  txtstream.WriteLine    ("<table    Border='0'    cellpadding='1'
cellspacing='1'>")

               End Select

            For x = 0 To rs.Fields.Count - 1

               Select Case ControlType

                  Case "Button"
                  txtstream.WriteLine ("<td style='font-family:Calibri, Sans-Serif;font-
size:    12px;color:navy;'><input    type=button    datasrc=#rs    datafld='"    &
rs.Fields(x).Name & "'></input></td>")
                  Case "Combobox"
```

```
            txtstream.WriteLine ("<td style='font-family:Calibri, Sans-Serif;font-
size: 12px;color:navy;'><select datasrc=#rs datafld='" & rs.Fields(x).Name &
"'></select></td>")
                    Case "Div"
            txtstream.WriteLine ("<td style='font-family:Calibri, Sans-Serif;font-
size: 12px;color:navy;'><div datasrc=#rs datafld='" & rs.Fields(x).Name &
"'></div></td>")
                    Case "Listbox"
            txtstream.WriteLine ("<td style='font-family:Calibri, Sans-Serif;font-
size: 12px;color:navy;'><select multiple=true datasrc=#rs datafld='" &
rs.Fields(x).Name & "'></option></select></td>")
                    Case "Span"
            txtstream.WriteLine ("<td style='font-family:Calibri, Sans-Serif;font-
size: 12px;color:navy;'><span datasrc=#rs datafld='" & rs.Fields(x).Name &
"'></span></td>")
                    Case "Textbox"
            txtstream.WriteLine ("<td style='font-family:Calibri, Sans-Serif;font-
size: 12px;color:navy;'><input type=text datasrc=#rs datafld='" & rs.Fields(x).Name
& "'></input></td>")
                    Case "Textarea"
            txtstream.WriteLine ("<td style='font-family:Calibri, Sans-Serif;font-
size: 12px;color:navy;'><textarea datasrc=#rs datafld='" & rs.Fields(x).Name &
"'></textarea></td>")

            End Select

        Next


        End Select

    Else

    Select Case Orientation


        Case "Single-Line Horizontal"

        Select Case TableType
```

```vb
            Case "Table"

                txtstream.WriteLine    ("<table    Border='1'    cellpadding='1'
cellspacing='1'>")

            Case "Report"

                txtstream.WriteLine    ("<table    Border='0'    cellpadding='1'
cellspacing='1'>")

        End Select


        txtstream.WriteLine ("<tr>")
        For x = 0 To rs.Fields.Count - 1

            txtstream.WriteLine ("<th >" & rs.Fields(x).Name & "</th>")

        Next
        txtstream.WriteLine ("</tr>")
        txtstream.WriteLine ("<tr>")
        For x = 0 To rs.Fields.Count - 1

            Select Case ControlType

                Case "Button"
                txtstream.WriteLine ("<td ><input type=button datasrc=#rs datafld='"
& rs.Fields(x).Name & "'></input></td>")
                Case "Combobox"
                txtstream.WriteLine    ("<td    ><select    datasrc=#rs    datafld='"    &
rs.Fields(x).Name & "'></select></td>")
                Case "Div"
                txtstream.WriteLine    ("<td    ><div    datasrc=#rs    datafld='"    &
rs.Fields(x).Name & "'></div></td>")
                Case "Listbox"
                txtstream.WriteLine    ("<td    ><select    multiple=true    datasrc=#rs
datafld='" & rs.Fields(x).Name & "'></option></select></td>")
                Case "Span"
                txtstream.WriteLine    ("<td    ><span    datasrc=#rs    datafld='"    &
rs.Fields(x).Name & "'></span></td>")
```

```
                    Case "Textbox"
            txtstream.WriteLine ("<td ><input type=text datasrc=#rs datafld='" &
rs.Fields(x).Name & "'></input></td>")
                    Case "Textarea"
            txtstream.WriteLine ("<td ><textarea datasrc=#rs datafld='" &
rs.Fields(x).Name & "'></textarea></td>")

            End Select



        Next

            txtstream.WriteLine ("</tr>")



    Case "Multi-Line Horizontal"


        Select Case TableType

            Case "Table"

                txtstream.WriteLine   ("<table   Border='1'   cellpadding='1'
cellspacing='1' datasrc=#rs>")

            Case "Report"

                txtstream.WriteLine   ("<table   Border='0'   cellpadding='1'
cellspacing='1' datasrc=#rs>")

        End Select

        txtstream.WriteLine ("<thead><tr>")
        For x = 0 To rs.Fields.Count - 1

            txtstream.WriteLine ("<th >" & rs.Fields(x).Name & "</th>")

        Next
        txtstream.WriteLine ("</tr></thead>")
```

```vb
        txtstream.WriteLine ("<tbody><tr>")
        For x = 0 To rs.Fields.Count - 1

            Select Case ControlType

                Case "Button"
                txtstream.WriteLine ("<td ><input type=button datasrc=#rs datafld='"
& rs.Fields(x).Name & "'></input></td>")
                Case "Combobox"
                txtstream.WriteLine ("<td ><select datasrc=#rs datafld='" &
rs.Fields(x).Name & "'></select></td>")
                Case "Div"
                txtstream.WriteLine ("<td ><div datasrc=#rs datafld='" &
rs.Fields(x).Name & "'></div></td>")
                Case "Listbox"
                txtstream.WriteLine ("<td ><select multiple=true datasrc=#rs
datafld='" & rs.Fields(x).Name & "'></option></select></td>")
                Case "Span"
                txtstream.WriteLine ("<td ><span datasrc=#rs datafld='" &
rs.Fields(x).Name & "'></span></td>")
                Case "Textbox"
                txtstream.WriteLine ("<td ><input type=text datasrc=#rs datafld='" &
rs.Fields(x).Name & "'></input></td>")
                Case "Textarea"
                txtstream.WriteLine ("<td ><textarea datasrc=#rs datafld='" &
rs.Fields(x).Name & "'></textarea></td>")

            End Select

        Next

            txtstream.WriteLine ("</tr></tbody>")



    Case "Single-Line Vertical"


        Select Case TableType
```

```
Case "Table"

        txtstream.WriteLine      ("<table    Border='1'   cellpadding='1'
cellspacing='1'>")

    Case "Report"

        txtstream.WriteLine      ("<table    Border='0'   cellpadding='1'
cellspacing='1'>")

    End Select

    For x = 0 To rs.Fields.Count - 1

    Select Case ControlType

        Case "Button"
    txtstream.WriteLine ("<td ><input type=button datasrc=#rs datafld='"
& rs.Fields(x).Name & "'></input></td>")
        Case "Combobox"
    txtstream.WriteLine    ("<td    ><select   datasrc=#rs   datafld='"   &
rs.Fields(x).Name & "'></select></td>")
        Case "Div"
    txtstream.WriteLine    ("<td    ><div    datasrc=#rs   datafld='"   &
rs.Fields(x).Name & "'></div></td>")
        Case "Listbox"
    txtstream.WriteLine    ("<td    ><select   multiple=true   datasrc=#rs
datafld='" & rs.Fields(x).Name & "'></option></select></td>")
        Case "Span"
    txtstream.WriteLine    ("<td    ><span   datasrc=#rs   datafld='"   &
rs.Fields(x).Name & "'></span></td>")
        Case "Textbox"
    txtstream.WriteLine ("<td ><input type=text datasrc=#rs datafld='" &
rs.Fields(x).Name & "'></input></td>")
        Case "Textarea"
    txtstream.WriteLine   ("<td    ><textarea   datasrc=#rs   datafld='"   &
rs.Fields(x).Name & "'></textarea></td>")

    End Select
```

```
        Next


     End Select



   End If

   txtstream.WriteLine ("</table>")
   txtstream.WriteLine ("</body>")
   txtstream.WriteLine ("</html>")
   txtstream.Close




   tempstr = ""
   Set txtstream = fso.OpenTextFile(ws.CurrentDirectory & "\" & Tablename &
".html", 1, True, -2)
     Do While txtstream.AtEndOfStream = False
        tempstr = tempstr & txtstream.ReadLine()
        tempstr = tempstr & vbCrLf
     Loop
     txtstream.Close
     textarea1.innerText = tempstr



 End Sub

 Sub LT1_OnClick()

   If fName.Value = "" then
        msgbox("Please provide the location and name of the database you want to
use before clicking here.")
        exit sub
   else
        cnstr = "Provider=" & Provider & ";Data Source = " & FName.Value & ";"

        Set cn = CreateObject("ADODB.Connection")
```

```
On Error Resume Next
cn.ConnectionString = cnstr
Call cn.Open()
if err.number = 0 then
    Set ws = CreateObject("WScript.Shell")
    Set fso = CreateObject("Scripting.FileSystemObject")
    Set txtstream = fso.OpenTextFile(ws.CurrentDirectory & "\tables.txt", 2,
true, -2)
    Set rs1 = cn.OpenSchema(20)
    Dim l()
    Redim l(3)
    l(0) = Len("Tablename")
    l(1) = Len("TableType")
    l(2) = Len("Description")

    Do While rs1.EOF = false
        if len(rs1.Fields("TABLE_NAME").Value) > l(0) then
            l(0) = len(rs1.Fields("TABLE_NAME").Value)
        End If

        if len(rs1.Fields("TABLE_TYPE").Value) > l(1) then
            l(1) = len(rs1.Fields("TABLE_TYPE").Value)
        End If

        if len(rs1.Fields("TABLE_DESCRIPTION").Value) > l(2) then
            l(2) = len(rs1.Fields("TABLE_DESCRIPTION").Value)
        End If

        rs1.MoveNext
    Loop

    rs1.MoveFirst

    l(0) = l(0) + 3
    l(1) = l(1) + 3
    l(2) = l(2) + 3

    Dim v

    v = l(0) - Len("Tablename")
```

```
mystr = "Tablename" & space(v)
v = l(1) - Len("TableType")
mystr = mystr & "TableType" & space(v)
v = l(2) - Len("Description")
mystr = mystr & "Description" & space(v)
txtstream.WriteLine(mystr)
mystr = ""
txtstream.WriteLine("")

Set tbl = document.GetElementByID("trex")
tbl.innerHTML = ""
Set opt = document.createElement("option")
opt.value = "*Select An Option*"
opt.text = "*Select An Option*"
opt.Selected = true
tbl.Options.Add(opt)




Do While rs1.EOF = false



    If mid(rs1.Fields("TABLE_NAME").Value, 1,4) <> "MSys" then

      If rs1.Fields("TABLE_TYPE").Value = "TABLE" then
        Set opt = document.createElement("option")
        opt.value = rs1.Fields("TABLE_NAME").Value
        opt.text = rs1.Fields("TABLE_NAME").Value
        tbl.Options.Add(opt)
      End If

          v = l(0) - Len(rs1.Fields("TABLE_NAME").Value)
          mystr = rs1.Fields("TABLE_NAME").Value & space(v)
          v = l(1) - Len(rs1.Fields("TABLE_TYPE").Value)
          mystr = mystr & rs1.Fields("TABLE_TYPE").Value & space(v)
          v = l(2) - Len(rs1.Fields("DESCRIPTION").Value)
          mystr = mystr & rs1.Fields("DESCRIPTION").Value
          txtstream.WriteLine(mystr)
          mystr = ""
```

```
            End If
            rs1.MoveNext
         Loop

         Dim tempstr
         tempstr = ""
         Set txtstream = fso.OpenTextFile(ws.CurrentDirectory & "\tables.txt", 1,
true, -2)
         Do While txtstream.AtEndOfStream = false
            tempstr = tempstr & txtstream.ReadLine()
            tempstr = tempstr & vbcrlf
         loop
         txtstream.Close
         textarea1.innerText = tempstr
      Else

         msgbox("Test connection Failed with: " & err.Description)

      End IF

   End If

   strQuery = ""

End Sub

Sub TestConnection1_OnClick()

   If fName.Value = "" then
      msgbox("Please provide the location and name of the database you want to
use before clicking here.")
      exit sub
   else
      cnstr = "Provider=" & Provider & ";Data Source = " & FName.Value & ";"
      Set cn = CreateObject("ADODB.Connection")
      On Error Resume Next
      cn.ConnectionString = cnstr
      Call cn.Open()
      if err.number = 0 then
         msgbox("Test connection succeeded.")
```

```vbscript
        else
            msgbox("Connecion failed with: " & err.Description)
        End If
    End If

End Sub

Sub Search_OnClick()

    Set ws = CreateObject("WScript.Shell")
    Set OpenDialog1 = CreateObject("MSComDlg.CommonDialog")

    With OpenDialog1
        .DialogTitle = "Open Database"
        .InitDir = ws.CurrentDirectory
        .Filter = "Microsoft Older Access Database(*.mdb)|*.mdb|Microsoft Newer
Access Database(*.accdb)|*.accdb"
        .FilterIndex = 2
        .MaxFileSize =32000
        .Flags = 2621952
        .ShowOpen
    End With
    If OpenDialog1.Filename <> "" then
        FName.Value = OpenDialog1.Filename
    End If

End Sub

Sub DataLinks1_OnClick()

    Set cn = createObject("ADODB.Connection")
    Set dl = CreateObject("Datalinks")
    Set cn = dl.PromptNew()
    Provider= cn.Provider
    cnstr = cn.ConnectionString
    FName.Value = cn.Properties("Data Source").Value

End Sub

Sub Clipboard1_OnClick()
```

```
      Set range = Textarea1.createTextRange()
      call range.findText(Textarea1.InnerText)
      range.select
      Call document.execCommand("Copy")
      Call document.execCommand("Unselect")

   End Sub

   Sub RunMe_OnClick()

      Set ws = CreateObject("WScript.Shell")
      Set fso = CreateObject("Scripting.FileSystemObject")

      Set txtstream = fso.OpenTextFile(ws.CurrentDirectory & "\" & Tablename &
".vbs", 2, true, -2)
      txtstream.WriteLine(Textarea1.innerText)
      txtstream.Close()
      Set txtstream = nothing
      Dim shorty
      Shorty = fso.GetFolder(ws.CurrentDirectory).ShortPath
      call ws.Run("C:\Windows\SysWOW64\wscript.exe " & Shorty & "\Code.vbs")
      Set fso = nothing

   End Sub

   Sub ViewMe_OnClick()

      Set ws = CreateObject("WScript.Shell")
      Set fso = CreateObject("Scripting.FileSystemObject")
      Dim shorty
      Shorty = fso.GetFolder(ws.CurrentDirectory).ShortPath
      Set txtstream = fso.OpenTextFile(shorty & "\" & Tablename & ".hta", 2, true, -
2)
      txtstream.WriteLine(Textarea1.innerText)
      txtstream.Close()
      call ws.Run(Shorty & "\" & Tablename & ".hta")
      Set fso = nothing
      Set ws = nothing
```

```
End Sub

Sub Document_OnClick()

End Sub

Sub wd_OnClick()

  Dim oWord
  Set range = Textarea1.createTextRange()
  Call range.findText(Textarea1.InnerText)
  range.Select
  Call Document.execCommand("Copy")
  Set oWordApp = CreateObject("Word.Application")
  oWordApp.Visible = True
  oWordApp.Activate
  Set oWord = oWordApp.Documents.Add()
  Set oParagraph = oWord.Application.ActiveDocument.Paragraphs.Add()
  oParagraph.Alignment = wdAlignParagraphJustify
  oParagraph.range.Font.Name = "Merriweather"
  oParagraph.range.Font.Size = 8
  oParagraph.CharacterUnitFirstLineIndent = 0.3
  oParagraph.Format.LineSpacing = 1.5
  oParagraph.Format.LineUnitBefore = 0
  oParagraph.Format.LineUnitAfter = 0
  oParagraph.range.PasteAndFormat (22)
  Call Document.execCommand("Unselect")

End Sub

Sub EMail_OnClick()

  if sn.Value = "" Then
     msgbox("Please enter the name of the mail server you want to connect to
before clicking here.")
     Exit Sub
  End If

  if lnu.Value = "" Then
```

```
        msgbox("Please enter your Logon name you use to log into mail server to
before clicking here.")
        Exit Sub
    End If

    if lpwd.Value = "" Then
        msgbox("Please enter your Logon password you use to log into mail server to
before clicking here.")
        Exit Sub
    End If

    if emfn.Value = "" Then
        msgbox("Please enter the user friendly name you use send and receive mail
before clicking here.")
        Exit Sub
    End If

    if ema.Value = "" Then
        msgbox("Please enter your email address you use send and receive mail before
clicking here.")
        Exit Sub
    End If

    if rec.Value = "" Then
        msgbox("Please enter the email address of the person you want to send this
mail to before clicking here.")
        Exit Sub
    End If

    if s.Value = "" Then
        msgbox("Please enter a subject or title you want to use with this mail before
clicking here.")
        Exit Sub
    End If


    Dim SMTPServer
    Dim SMTPLogon
    Dim LogonUserName
    Dim LogonPassword
```

```
Dim strHTML
Dim shorty
Set ws = CreateObject("WScript.Shell")
Set fso = CreateObject("Scripting.FileSystemObject")
Shorty = fso.GetFolder(ws.CurrentDirectory).ShortPath
Set txtstream = fso.OpenTextFile(shorty & "\" & Tablename & ".hta", 1, true, -
2)
Do While txtstream.AtEndOfStream = false
   strHTML = strHTML & txtstream.ReadLine()
   strHTML = strHTML & vbcrlf
Loop
txtstream.Close()

EMailFrom = ema.Value
EmailFromName = emfn.Value
EmailTo = rec.Value
SMTPServer = sn.Value
SMTPLogon = lnu.Value
SMTPPassword = lpwd.Value




Const SMTPSSL = True
Const SMTPPort = 465

Const cdoSendUsingPickup = 1   'Send message using local SMTP service pickup
directory.
Const cdoSendUsingPort = 2     'Send the message using SMTP over TCP/IP
networking.

Const cdoAnonymous = 0      ' No authentication
Const cdoBasic = 1      ' BASIC clear text authentication
Const cdoNTLM = 2      ' NTLM, Microsoft proprietary authentication

' First, create the message

Set objMessage = CreateObject("CDO.Message")
objMessage.Subject = s.Value
objMessage.From = """" & EmailFromName & """" <" & EmailFrom & ">"
```

```
objMessage.To = EmailTo
objMessage.HTMLBody = strHTML

' Second, configure the server

objMessage.Configuration.Fields.Item("http://schemas.microsoft.com/cdo/config
uration/sendusing") = 2
objMessage.Configuration.Fields.Item("http://schemas.microsoft.com/cdo/config
uration/smtpusessl") = true
objMessage.Configuration.Fields.Item("http://schemas.microsoft.com/cdo/config
uration/smtpserver") = SMTPServer
objMessage.Configuration.Fields.Item("http://schemas.microsoft.com/cdo/config
uration/smtpauthenticate") = cdoBasic
objMessage.Configuration.Fields.Item("http://schemas.microsoft.com/cdo/config
uration/sendusername") = SMTPLogon
objMessage.Configuration.Fields.Item("http://schemas.microsoft.com/cdo/config
uration/sendpassword") = SMTPPassword
objMessage.Configuration.Fields.Item("http://schemas.microsoft.com/cdo/config
uration/smtpserverport") = SMTPPort
objMessage.Configuration.Fields.Item("http://schemas.microsoft.com/cdo/config
uration/smtpconnectiontimeout") = 60
Call objMessage.Configuration.Fields.Update()

On Error Resume Next

Call objMessage.Send()

If err.Number = 0 then

    Msgbox("Your message has been sent successfully!")

else

    Msgbox("Unable to send the mail. Error Message: " & err.Description)

    err.Clear

End If

End Sub
```

```
Sub Providers_OnClick()

    Const HKEY_LOCAL_MACHINE = &H80000002
    strComputer = "."
    Dim strValue
    Set                    oReg                    =
GetObject("winmgmts:{impersonationLevel=impersonate}!\\.\root\default:StdRegPr
ov")
        oReg.EnumKey                    HKEY_LOCAL_MACHINE,
"SOFTWARE\Wow6432Node\Classes\CLSID", SubKeyNames
        mystr       =         "Providers       found        in
HKEY_LOCAL_MACHINE\SOFTWARE\Wow6432Node\Classes\CLSID" & vbCrLf
        For Each skn In SubKeyNames
            If                    oReg.GetStringValue(HKEY_LOCAL_MACHINE,
"SOFTWARE\Wow6432Node\Classes\CLSID\" & skn & "\Ole Db Provider", "",
strValue) = 0 Then
                oReg.GetStringValue                    HKEY_LOCAL_MACHINE,
"SOFTWARE\Wow6432Node\Classes\CLSID\" & skn, "", strValue
            mystr = mystr & strValue & vbCrLf
        End If
    Next
    mystr = mystr & "" & vbCrLf
    Textarea1.innerText = mystr

End Sub

Sub Drivers_OnClick()

    const HKEY_LOCAL_MACHINE = &H80000002
    strComputer = "."
    Set                                        oReg=
GetObject("winmgmts:{impersonationLevel=impersonate}!\\.\root\default:StdRegPr
ov")

    if              oReg.EnumValues              (HKEY_LOCAL_MACHINE,
"SOFTWARE\Wow6432Node\ODBC\ODBCINST.INI\ODBC Drivers", SubKeyNames) =
0 Then
```

```
      mystr              =              "Drivers            found            in
HKEY_LOCAL_MACHINE\SOFTWARE\Wow6432Node\ODBC\ODBCINST.INI\ODBC
Drivers" & vbcrlf
      mystr = mystr & "" & vbcrlf
      for each skn in SubKeyNames
         mystr = mystr & skn & vbcrlf
      Next
      mystr = mystr & "" & vbcrlf
      Textarea1.innerText = mystr
   End If

   End Sub

   Sub ISAMS_OnClick()

   Dim tempstr
   Dim SubKeyNames

   const HKEY_LOCAL_MACHINE = &H80000002
   strComputer = "."
   Set                                                                    oreg=
GetObject("winmgmts:{impersonationLevel=impersonate}!\\.\root\default:StdRegPr
ov")
      if                          oreg.EnumKey(HKEY_LOCAL_MACHINE,
"SOFTWARE\Wow6432Node\Microsoft\Jet 3.5\ISAM Formats", SubKeyNames) = 0
then
      mystr          =          "Found      Jet      3.5      ISAMS      in
HKEY_LOCAL_MACHINE\Wow6432Node\Microsoft\Jet 3.5\ISAM Formats" & vbcrlf
      mystr = mystr & "" & vbcrlf
      for each skn in SubKeyNames
         mystr = mystr & skn & vbcrlf
      Next
      mystr = mystr & "" & vbcrlf
   End If

      if                          oreg.EnumKey(HKEY_LOCAL_MACHINE,
"SOFTWARE\Wow6432Node\Microsoft\Jet 4.0\ISAM Formats", SubKeyNames) = 0
then
      mystr     =     mystr     &     "Found      Jet      4.0      ISAMS      in
HKEY_LOCAL_MACHINE\Wow6432Node\Microsoft\Jet 4.0\ISAM Formats" & vbcrlf
```

```
    mystr = mystr & "" & vbcrlf
    for each skn in SubKeyNames
        mystr = mystr & skn & vbcrlf
    Next
    mystr = mystr & "" & vbcrlf
End If


    if                              oReg.EnumKey(HKEY_LOCAL_MACHINE,
"SOFTWARE\Wow6432Node\Microsoft\Office\10.0\Access Connectivity Engine\ISAM
Formats", SubKeyNames) = 0 then
    mystr    =    mystr    &    "Found    ACE    10.0    ISAMS    in
SOFTWARE\Wow6432Node\Microsoft\Office\10.0\Access  Connectivity  Engine\ISAM
Formats" & vbcrlf
    mystr = mystr & "" & vbcrlf
    for each skn in SubKeyNames
        mystr = mystr & skn & vbcrlf
    Next
    mystr = mystr & "" & vbcrlf
End If


    if                              oReg.EnumKey(HKEY_LOCAL_MACHINE,
"SOFTWARE\Wow6432Node\Microsoft\Office\12.0\Access  Connectivity  Engine\ISAM
Formats", SubKeyNames) = 0 then
    mystr    =    mystr    &    "Found    ACE    12.0    ISAMS    in
KEY_LOCAL_MACHHINE\SOFTWARE\Wow6432Node\Microsoft\Office\12.0\Access
Connectivity Engine\ISAM Formats" & vbcrlf
    mystr = mystr & "" & vbcrlf
    for each skn in SubKeyNames
        mystr = mystr & skn & vbcrlf
    Next
    mystr = mystr & "" & vbcrlf
End If


    if                              oReg.EnumKey(HKEY_LOCAL_MACHINE,
"SOFTWARE\Wow6432Node\Microsoft\Office\14.0\Access  Connectivity  Engine\ISAM
Formats", SubKeyNames) = 0 then
    mystr    =    mystr    &    "Found    ACE    14.0    ISAMS    in
KEY_LOCAL_MACHHINE\SOFTWARE\Wow6432Node\Microsoft\Office\14.0\Access
Connectivity Engine\ISAM Formats" & vbcrlf
    mystr = mystr & "" & vbcrlf
```

```
      for each skn in SubKeyNames
         mystr = mystr & skn & vbcrlf
      Next
      mystr = mystr & "" & vbcrlf
   End If


   if                                    oReg.EnumKey(HKEY_LOCAL_MACHINE,
"SOFTWARE\Wow6432Node\Microsoft\Office\15.0\Access Connectivity Engine\ISAM
Formats", SubKeyNames) = 0 then
      mystr   =   mystr   &   "Found   ACE   15.0   ISAMS   in
KEY_LOCAL_MACHHINE\SOFTWARE\Wow6432Node\Microsoft\Office\15.0\Access
Connectivity Engine\ISAM Formats" & vbcrlf
      mystr = mystr & "" & vbcrlf
      for each skn in SubKeyNames
         mystr = mystr & skn & vbcrlf
      Next
      mystr = mystr & "" & vbcrlf
   End If


   if                                    oReg.EnumKey(HKEY_LOCAL_MACHINE,
"SOFTWARE\Wow6432Node\Microsoft\Office\16.0\Access Connectivity Engine\ISAM
Formats", SubKeyNames) = 0 then
      mystr   =   mystr   &   "Found   ACE   16.0   ISAMS   in
KEY_LOCAL_MACHHINE\SOFTWARE\Wow6432Node\Microsoft\Office\16.0\Access
Connectivity Engine\ISAM Formats" & vbcrlf
      mystr = mystr & "" & vbcrlf
      for each skn in SubKeyNames
         mystr = mystr & skn & vbcrlf
      Next
      mystr = mystr & "" & vbcrlf
   End If


   Textarea1.innerText = mystr

   End Sub

   Sub Create_Template()

   End Sub
```

```
Sub Add_The_StyleSheet()

    Select Case StyleSheet

        Case "None"

        Case "Basic"

            txtstream.WriteLine("<style type='text/css'>")
            txtstream.WriteLine("th")
            txtstream.WriteLine("{")
            txtstream.WriteLine("   COLOR: Darkred;")
            txtstream.WriteLine("}")
            txtstream.WriteLine("td")
            txtstream.WriteLine("{")
            txtstream.WriteLine("   COLOR: navy;")
            txtstream.WriteLine("}")
            txtstream.WriteLine("</style>")

        Case "InLine"


        Case "Table"

            txtstream.WriteLine("<style type=text/css>")
            txtstream.WriteLine("#itsthetable {")
            txtstream.WriteLine(" font-family:    Georgia,    """"""Times    New
Roman"""""", Times, serif;")
            txtstream.WriteLine(" color: #036;")
            txtstream.WriteLine("}")

            txtstream.WriteLine("caption {")
            txtstream.WriteLine(" font-size: 48px;")
            txtstream.WriteLine(" color: #036;")
            txtstream.WriteLine(" font-weight: bolder;")
            txtstream.WriteLine(" font-variant: small-caps;")
            txtstream.WriteLine("}")
```

```
txtstream.WriteLine("th {")
txtstream.WriteLine(" font-size: 12px;")
txtstream.WriteLine(" color: #FFF;")
txtstream.WriteLine(" background-color: #06C;")
txtstream.WriteLine(" padding: 8px 4px;")
txtstream.WriteLine(" border-bottom: 1px solid #015ebc;")
txtstream.WriteLine("}")

txtstream.WriteLine("table {")
txtstream.WriteLine(" margin: 0;")
txtstream.WriteLine(" padding: 0;")
txtstream.WriteLine(" border-collapse: collapse;")
txtstream.WriteLine(" border: 1px solid #06C;")
txtstream.WriteLine(" width: 100%")
txtstream.WriteLine("}")

txtstream.WriteLine("#itsthetable th a:link, #itsthetable th a:visited {")
txtstream.WriteLine(" color: #FFF;")
txtstream.WriteLine(" text-decoration: none;")
txtstream.WriteLine(" border-left: 5px solid #FFF;")
txtstream.WriteLine(" padding-left: 3px;")
txtstream.WriteLine("}")

txtstream.WriteLine("th a:hover, #itsthetable th a:active {")
txtstream.WriteLine(" color: #F90;")
txtstream.WriteLine(" text-decoration: line-through;")
txtstream.WriteLine(" border-left: 5px solid #F90;")
txtstream.WriteLine(" padding-left: 3px;")
txtstream.WriteLine("}")

txtstream.WriteLine("tbody th:hover {")
txtstream.WriteLine(" background-image: url(imgs/tbody_hover.gif);")
txtstream.WriteLine(" background-position: bottom;")
txtstream.WriteLine(" background-repeat: repeat-x;")
txtstream.WriteLine("}")

txtstream.WriteLine("td {")
txtstream.WriteLine(" background-color: #f2f2f2;")
```

```
txtstream.WriteLine(" padding: 4px;")
txtstream.WriteLine(" font-size: 12px;")
txtstream.WriteLine("}")

txtstream.WriteLine("#itsthetable td:hover {")
txtstream.WriteLine(" background-color: #f8f8f8;")

txtstream.WriteLine("}")

txtstream.WriteLine("#itsthetable td a:link, #itsthetable td a:visited {")
txtstream.WriteLine(" color: #039;")
txtstream.WriteLine(" text-decoration: none;")
txtstream.WriteLine(" border-left: 3px solid #039;")
txtstream.WriteLine(" padding-left: 3px;")
txtstream.WriteLine("}")

txtstream.WriteLine("#itsthetable td a:hover, #itsthetable td a:active {")
txtstream.WriteLine(" color: #06C;")
txtstream.WriteLine(" text-decoration: line-through;")
txtstream.WriteLine(" border-left: 3px solid #06C;")
txtstream.WriteLine(" padding-left: 3px;")
txtstream.WriteLine("}")

txtstream.WriteLine("#itsthetable th {")
txtstream.WriteLine(" text-align: left;")
txtstream.WriteLine(" width: 150px;")
txtstream.WriteLine("}")

txtstream.WriteLine("#itsthetable tr {")
txtstream.WriteLine(" border-bottom: 1px solid #CCC;")
txtstream.WriteLine("}")

txtstream.WriteLine("#itsthetable thead th {")
txtstream.WriteLine(" background-image: url(imgs/thead_back.gif);")
txtstream.WriteLine(" background-repeat: repeat-x;")
txtstream.WriteLine(" background-color: #06C;")
txtstream.WriteLine(" height: 30px;")
txtstream.WriteLine(" font-size: 18px;")
txtstream.WriteLine(" text-align: center;")
```

```
txtstream.WriteLine(" text-shadow: #333 2px 2px;")
txtstream.WriteLine(" border: 2px;")
txtstream.WriteLine("}")

txtstream.WriteLine("#itsthetable tfoot th {")
txtstream.WriteLine(" background-image: url(imgs/tfoot_back.gif);")
txtstream.WriteLine(" background-repeat: repeat-x;")
txtstream.WriteLine(" background-color: #036;")
txtstream.WriteLine(" height: 30px;")
txtstream.WriteLine(" font-size: 28px;")
txtstream.WriteLine(" text-align: center;")
txtstream.WriteLine(" text-shadow: #333 2px 2px;")
txtstream.WriteLine("}")

txtstream.WriteLine("#itsthetable tfoot td {")
txtstream.WriteLine(" background-image: url(imgs/tfoot_back.gif);")
txtstream.WriteLine(" background-repeat: repeat-x;")
txtstream.WriteLine(" background-color: #036;")
txtstream.WriteLine(" color: FFF;")
txtstream.WriteLine(" height: 30px;")
txtstream.WriteLine(" font-size: 24px;")
txtstream.WriteLine(" text-align: left;")
txtstream.WriteLine(" text-shadow: #333 2px 2px;")
txtstream.WriteLine("}")

txtstream.WriteLine("tbody td a[href="""""http://www.csslab.cl/"""""]
{")
txtstream.WriteLine(" font-weight: bolder;")
txtstream.WriteLine("}")
txtstream.WriteLine("</style>")


Case "BlackAndWhiteText"

txtstream.WriteLine("<style type='text/css'>")
txtstream.WriteLine("th")
txtstream.WriteLine("{")
txtstream.WriteLine("    COLOR: white;")
txtstream.WriteLine("    BACKGROUND-COLOR: black;")
```

```
txtstream.WriteLine("   FONT-FAMILY:font-family: Cambria, serif;")
txtstream.WriteLine("   FONT-SIZE: 12px;")
txtstream.WriteLine("   text-align: left;")
txtstream.WriteLine("   white-Space: nowrap;")
txtstream.WriteLine("}")
txtstream.WriteLine("td")
txtstream.WriteLine("{")
txtstream.WriteLine("   COLOR: white;")
txtstream.WriteLine("   BACKGROUND-COLOR: black;")
txtstream.WriteLine("   FONT-FAMILY: font-family: Cambria, serif;")
txtstream.WriteLine("   FONT-SIZE: 12px;")
txtstream.WriteLine("   text-align: left;")
txtstream.WriteLine("   white-Space: nowrap;")
txtstream.WriteLine("}")
txtstream.WriteLine("div")
txtstream.WriteLine("{")
txtstream.WriteLine("   COLOR: white;")
txtstream.WriteLine("   BACKGROUND-COLOR: black;")
txtstream.WriteLine("   FONT-FAMILY: font-family: Cambria, serif;")
txtstream.WriteLine("   FONT-SIZE: 10px;")
txtstream.WriteLine("   text-align: left;")
txtstream.WriteLine("   white-Space: nowrap;")
txtstream.WriteLine("}")
txtstream.WriteLine("span")
txtstream.WriteLine("{")
txtstream.WriteLine("   COLOR: white;")
txtstream.WriteLine("   BACKGROUND-COLOR: black;")
txtstream.WriteLine("   FONT-FAMILY: font-family: Cambria, serif;")
txtstream.WriteLine("   FONT-SIZE: 10px;")
txtstream.WriteLine("   text-align: left;")
txtstream.WriteLine("   white-Space: nowrap;")
txtstream.WriteLine("   display:inline-block;")
txtstream.WriteLine("   width: 100%;")
txtstream.WriteLine("}")
txtstream.WriteLine("textarea")
txtstream.WriteLine("{")
txtstream.WriteLine("   COLOR: white;")
txtstream.WriteLine("   BACKGROUND-COLOR: black;")
txtstream.WriteLine("   FONT-FAMILY: font-family: Cambria, serif;")
txtstream.WriteLine("   FONT-SIZE: 10px;")
```

```
txtstream.WriteLine("    text-align: left;")
txtstream.WriteLine("    white-Space: nowrap;")
txtstream.WriteLine("    width: 100%;")
txtstream.WriteLine("}")
txtstream.WriteLine("select")
txtstream.WriteLine("{")
txtstream.WriteLine("    COLOR: white;")
txtstream.WriteLine("    BACKGROUND-COLOR: black;")
txtstream.WriteLine("    FONT-FAMILY: font-family: Cambria, serif;")
txtstream.WriteLine("    FONT-SIZE: 10px;")
txtstream.WriteLine("    text-align: left;")
txtstream.WriteLine("    white-Space: nowrap;")
txtstream.WriteLine("    width: 100%;")
txtstream.WriteLine("}")
txtstream.WriteLine("input")
txtstream.WriteLine("{")
txtstream.WriteLine("    COLOR: white;")
txtstream.WriteLine("    BACKGROUND-COLOR: black;")
txtstream.WriteLine("    FONT-FAMILY: font-family: Cambria, serif;")
txtstream.WriteLine("    FONT-SIZE: 12px;")
txtstream.WriteLine("    text-align: left;")
txtstream.WriteLine("    display:table-cell;")
txtstream.WriteLine("    white-Space: nowrap;")
txtstream.WriteLine("}")
txtstream.WriteLine("h1 {")
txtstream.WriteLine("color: antiquewhite;")
txtstream.WriteLine("text-shadow: 1px 1px 1px black;")
txtstream.WriteLine("padding: 3px;")
txtstream.WriteLine("text-align: center;")
txtstream.WriteLine("box-shadow: in2px 2px 5px rgba(0,0,0,0.5), in-
2px -2px 5px rgba(255,255,255,0.5);")
txtstream.WriteLine("}")
txtstream.WriteLine("</style>")

    Case "ColoredText"

txtstream.WriteLine("<style type='text/css'>")
txtstream.WriteLine("th")
txtstream.WriteLine("{")
txtstream.WriteLine("    COLOR: darkred;")
```

```
txtstream.WriteLine("    BACKGROUND-COLOR: #eeeeee;")
txtstream.WriteLine("    FONT-FAMILY:font-family: Cambria, serif;")
txtstream.WriteLine("    FONT-SIZE: 12px;")
txtstream.WriteLine("    text-align: left;")
txtstream.WriteLine("    white-Space: nowrap;")
txtstream.WriteLine("}")
txtstream.WriteLine("td")
txtstream.WriteLine("{")
txtstream.WriteLine("    COLOR: navy;")
txtstream.WriteLine("    BACKGROUND-COLOR: #eeeeee;")
txtstream.WriteLine("    FONT-FAMILY: font-family: Cambria, serif;")
txtstream.WriteLine("    FONT-SIZE: 12px;")
txtstream.WriteLine("    text-align: left;")
txtstream.WriteLine("    white-Space: nowrap;")
txtstream.WriteLine("}")
txtstream.WriteLine("div")
txtstream.WriteLine("{")
txtstream.WriteLine("    COLOR: white;")
txtstream.WriteLine("    BACKGROUND-COLOR: navy;")
txtstream.WriteLine("    FONT-FAMILY: font-family: Cambria, serif;")
txtstream.WriteLine("    FONT-SIZE: 10px;")
txtstream.WriteLine("    text-align: left;")
txtstream.WriteLine("    white-Space: nowrap;")
txtstream.WriteLine("}")
txtstream.WriteLine("span")
txtstream.WriteLine("{")
txtstream.WriteLine("    COLOR: white;")
txtstream.WriteLine("    BACKGROUND-COLOR: navy;")
txtstream.WriteLine("    FONT-FAMILY: font-family: Cambria, serif;")
txtstream.WriteLine("    FONT-SIZE: 10px;")
txtstream.WriteLine("    text-align: left;")
txtstream.WriteLine("    white-Space: nowrap;")
txtstream.WriteLine("    display:inline-block;")
txtstream.WriteLine("    width: 100%;")
txtstream.WriteLine("}")
txtstream.WriteLine("textarea")
txtstream.WriteLine("{")
txtstream.WriteLine("    COLOR: white;")
txtstream.WriteLine("    BACKGROUND-COLOR: navy;")
txtstream.WriteLine("    FONT-FAMILY: font-family: Cambria, serif;")
```

```
txtstream.WriteLine("    FONT-SIZE: 10px;")
txtstream.WriteLine("    text-align: left;")
txtstream.WriteLine("    white-Space: nowrap;")
txtstream.WriteLine("    width: 100%;")
txtstream.WriteLine("}")
txtstream.WriteLine("select")
txtstream.WriteLine("{")
txtstream.WriteLine("    COLOR: white;")
txtstream.WriteLine("    BACKGROUND-COLOR: navy;")
txtstream.WriteLine("    FONT-FAMILY: font-family: Cambria, serif;")
txtstream.WriteLine("    FONT-SIZE: 10px;")
txtstream.WriteLine("    text-align: left;")
txtstream.WriteLine("    white-Space: nowrap;")
txtstream.WriteLine("    width: 100%;")
txtstream.WriteLine("}")
txtstream.WriteLine("input")
txtstream.WriteLine("{")
txtstream.WriteLine("    COLOR: white;")
txtstream.WriteLine("    BACKGROUND-COLOR: navy;")
txtstream.WriteLine("    FONT-FAMILY: font-family: Cambria, serif;")
txtstream.WriteLine("    FONT-SIZE: 12px;")
txtstream.WriteLine("    text-align: left;")
txtstream.WriteLine("    display:table-cell;")
txtstream.WriteLine("    white-Space: nowrap;")
txtstream.WriteLine("}")
txtstream.WriteLine("h1 {")
txtstream.WriteLine("color: antiquewhite;")
txtstream.WriteLine("text-shadow: 1px 1px 1px black;")
txtstream.WriteLine("padding: 3px;")
txtstream.WriteLine("text-align: center;")
txtstream.WriteLine("box-shadow: in2px 2px 5px rgba(0,0,0,0.5), in-
2px -2px 5px rgba(255,255,255,0.5);")
txtstream.WriteLine("}")
txtstream.WriteLine("</style>")


        Case "OscillatingRowColors"


        txtstream.WriteLine("<style type='text/css'> ")
```

```
txtstream.WriteLine("th")
txtstream.WriteLine("{")
txtstream.WriteLine("    COLOR: white;")
txtstream.WriteLine("    BACKGROUND-COLOR: navy;")
txtstream.WriteLine("    FONT-FAMILY:font-family: Cambria, serif;")
txtstream.WriteLine("    FONT-SIZE: 12px;")
txtstream.WriteLine("    text-align: left;")
txtstream.WriteLine("    white-Space: nowrap;")
txtstream.WriteLine("}")
txtstream.WriteLine("td")
txtstream.WriteLine("{")
txtstream.WriteLine("    COLOR: navy;")
txtstream.WriteLine("    FONT-FAMILY: font-family: Cambria, serif;")
txtstream.WriteLine("    FONT-SIZE: 12px;")
txtstream.WriteLine("    text-align: left;")
txtstream.WriteLine("    white-Space: nowrap;")
txtstream.WriteLine("}")
txtstream.WriteLine("div")
txtstream.WriteLine("{")
txtstream.WriteLine("    COLOR: navy;")
txtstream.WriteLine("    FONT-FAMILY: font-family: Cambria, serif;")
txtstream.WriteLine("    FONT-SIZE: 12px;")
txtstream.WriteLine("    text-align: left;")
txtstream.WriteLine("    white-Space: nowrap;")
txtstream.WriteLine("}")
txtstream.WriteLine("span")
txtstream.WriteLine("{")
txtstream.WriteLine("    COLOR: navy;")
txtstream.WriteLine("    FONT-FAMILY: font-family: Cambria, serif;")
txtstream.WriteLine("    FONT-SIZE: 12px;")
txtstream.WriteLine("    text-align: left;")
txtstream.WriteLine("    white-Space: nowrap;")
txtstream.WriteLine("    width: 100%;")
txtstream.WriteLine("}")
txtstream.WriteLine("textarea")
txtstream.WriteLine("{")
txtstream.WriteLine("    COLOR: navy;")
txtstream.WriteLine("    FONT-FAMILY: font-family: Cambria, serif;")
txtstream.WriteLine("    FONT-SIZE: 12px;")
txtstream.WriteLine("    text-align: left;")
```

```
txtstream.WriteLine("    white-Space: nowrap;")
txtstream.WriteLine("    display:inline-block;")
txtstream.WriteLine("    width: 100%;")
txtstream.WriteLine("}")
txtstream.WriteLine("select")
txtstream.WriteLine("{")
txtstream.WriteLine("    COLOR: navy;")
txtstream.WriteLine("    FONT-FAMILY: font-family: Cambria, serif;")
txtstream.WriteLine("    FONT-SIZE: 10px;")
txtstream.WriteLine("    text-align: left;")
txtstream.WriteLine("    white-Space: nowrap;")
txtstream.WriteLine("    display:inline-block;")
txtstream.WriteLine("    width: 100%;")
txtstream.WriteLine("}")
txtstream.WriteLine("input")
txtstream.WriteLine("{")
txtstream.WriteLine("    COLOR: navy;")
txtstream.WriteLine("    FONT-FAMILY: font-family: Cambria, serif;")
txtstream.WriteLine("    FONT-SIZE: 12px;")
txtstream.WriteLine("    text-align: left;")
txtstream.WriteLine("    display:table-cell;")
txtstream.WriteLine("    white-Space: nowrap;")
txtstream.WriteLine("}")
txtstream.WriteLine("h1 {")
txtstream.WriteLine("color: antiquewhite;")
txtstream.WriteLine("text-shadow: 1px 1px 1px black;")
txtstream.WriteLine("padding: 3px;")
txtstream.WriteLine("text-align: center;")
txtstream.WriteLine("box-shadow: in2px 2px 5px rgba(0,0,0,0.5), in-
2px -2px 5px rgba(255,255,255,0.5);")
txtstream.WriteLine("}")
txtstream.WriteLine("tr:nth-child(even){background-color:#f2f2f2;}")
txtstream.WriteLine("tr:nth-child(odd){background-color:#cccccc;
color:#f2f2f2;}")
txtstream.WriteLine("</style>")

Case "GhostDecorated"

txtstream.WriteLine("<style type='text/css'>")
txtstream.WriteLine("th")
```

```
txtstream.WriteLine("{")
txtstream.WriteLine("   COLOR: black;")
txtstream.WriteLine("   BACKGROUND-COLOR: white;")
txtstream.WriteLine("   FONT-FAMILY:font-family: Cambria, serif;")
txtstream.WriteLine("   FONT-SIZE: 12px;")
txtstream.WriteLine("   text-align: left;")
txtstream.WriteLine("   white-Space: nowrap;")
txtstream.WriteLine("}")
txtstream.WriteLine("td")
txtstream.WriteLine("{")
txtstream.WriteLine("   COLOR: black;")
txtstream.WriteLine("   BACKGROUND-COLOR: white;")
txtstream.WriteLine("   FONT-FAMILY: font-family: Cambria, serif;")
txtstream.WriteLine("   FONT-SIZE: 12px;")
txtstream.WriteLine("   text-align: left;")
txtstream.WriteLine("   white-Space: nowrap;")
txtstream.WriteLine("}")
txtstream.WriteLine("div")
txtstream.WriteLine("{")
txtstream.WriteLine("   COLOR: black;")
txtstream.WriteLine("   BACKGROUND-COLOR: white;")
txtstream.WriteLine("   FONT-FAMILY: font-family: Cambria, serif;")
txtstream.WriteLine("   FONT-SIZE: 10px;")
txtstream.WriteLine("   text-align: left;")
txtstream.WriteLine("   white-Space: nowrap;")
txtstream.WriteLine("}")
txtstream.WriteLine("span")
txtstream.WriteLine("{")
txtstream.WriteLine("   COLOR: black;")
txtstream.WriteLine("   BACKGROUND-COLOR: white;")
txtstream.WriteLine("   FONT-FAMILY: font-family: Cambria, serif;")
txtstream.WriteLine("   FONT-SIZE: 10px;")
txtstream.WriteLine("   text-align: left;")
txtstream.WriteLine("   white-Space: nowrap;")
txtstream.WriteLine("   display:inline-block;")
txtstream.WriteLine("   width: 100%;")
txtstream.WriteLine("}")
txtstream.WriteLine("textarea")
txtstream.WriteLine("{")
txtstream.WriteLine("   COLOR: black;")
```

```
txtstream.WriteLine("    BACKGROUND-COLOR: white;")
txtstream.WriteLine("    FONT-FAMILY: font-family: Cambria, serif;")
txtstream.WriteLine("    FONT-SIZE: 10px;")
txtstream.WriteLine("    text-align: left;")
txtstream.WriteLine("    white-Space: nowrap;")
txtstream.WriteLine("    width: 100%;")
txtstream.WriteLine("}")
txtstream.WriteLine("select")
txtstream.WriteLine("{")
txtstream.WriteLine("    COLOR: black;")
txtstream.WriteLine("    BACKGROUND-COLOR: white;")
txtstream.WriteLine("    FONT-FAMILY: font-family: Cambria, serif;")
txtstream.WriteLine("    FONT-SIZE: 10px;")
txtstream.WriteLine("    text-align: left;")
txtstream.WriteLine("    white-Space: nowrap;")
txtstream.WriteLine("    width: 100%;")
txtstream.WriteLine("}")
txtstream.WriteLine("input")
txtstream.WriteLine("{")
txtstream.WriteLine("    COLOR: black;")
txtstream.WriteLine("    BACKGROUND-COLOR: white;")
txtstream.WriteLine("    FONT-FAMILY: font-family: Cambria, serif;")
txtstream.WriteLine("    FONT-SIZE: 12px;")
txtstream.WriteLine("    text-align: left;")
txtstream.WriteLine("    display:table-cell;")
txtstream.WriteLine("    white-Space: nowrap;")
txtstream.WriteLine("}")
txtstream.WriteLine("h1 {")
txtstream.WriteLine("color: antiquewhite;")
txtstream.WriteLine("text-shadow: 1px 1px 1px black;")
txtstream.WriteLine("padding: 3px;")
txtstream.WriteLine("text-align: center;")
txtstream.WriteLine("box-shadow: in2px 2px 5px rgba(0,0,0,0.5), in-
2px -2px 5px rgba(255,255,255,0.5);")
txtstream.WriteLine("}")
txtstream.WriteLine("</style>")

        Case "3D"
```

```
txtstream.WriteLine("<style type='text/css'>")
txtstream.WriteLine("body")
txtstream.WriteLine("{")
txtstream.WriteLine("   PADDING-RIGHT: 0px;")
txtstream.WriteLine("   PADDING-LEFT: 0px;")
txtstream.WriteLine("   PADDING-BOTTOM: 0px;")
txtstream.WriteLine("   MARGIN: 0px;")
txtstream.WriteLine("   COLOR: #333;")
txtstream.WriteLine("   PADDING-TOP: 0px;")
txtstream.WriteLine("   FONT-FAMILY: verdana, arial, helvetica, sans-
serif;")
txtstream.WriteLine("}")
txtstream.WriteLine("table")
txtstream.WriteLine("{")
txtstream.WriteLine("   BORDER-RIGHT: #999999 3px solid;")
txtstream.WriteLine("   PADDING-RIGHT: 6px;")
txtstream.WriteLine("   PADDING-LEFT: 6px;")
txtstream.WriteLine("   FONT-WEIGHT: Bold;")
txtstream.WriteLine("   FONT-SIZE: 14px;")
txtstream.WriteLine("   PADDING-BOTTOM: 6px;")
txtstream.WriteLine("   COLOR: Peru;")
txtstream.WriteLine("   LINE-HEIGHT: 14px;")
txtstream.WriteLine("   PADDING-TOP: 6px;")
txtstream.WriteLine("   BORDER-BOTTOM: #999 1px solid;")
txtstream.WriteLine("   BACKGROUND-COLOR: #eeeeee;")
txtstream.WriteLine("   FONT-FAMILY: verdana, arial, helvetica, sans-
serif;")
txtstream.WriteLine("   FONT-SIZE: 12px;")
txtstream.WriteLine("}")
txtstream.WriteLine("th")
txtstream.WriteLine("{")
txtstream.WriteLine("   BORDER-RIGHT: #999999 3px solid;")
txtstream.WriteLine("   PADDING-RIGHT: 6px;")
txtstream.WriteLine("   PADDING-LEFT: 6px;")
txtstream.WriteLine("   FONT-WEIGHT: Bold;")
txtstream.WriteLine("   FONT-SIZE: 14px;")
txtstream.WriteLine("   PADDING-BOTTOM: 6px;")
txtstream.WriteLine("   COLOR: darkred;")
txtstream.WriteLine("   LINE-HEIGHT: 14px;")
txtstream.WriteLine("   PADDING-TOP: 6px;")
```

```
txtstream.WriteLine("    BORDER-BOTTOM: #999 1px solid;")
txtstream.WriteLine("    BACKGROUND-COLOR: #eeeeee;")
txtstream.WriteLine("    FONT-FAMILY:font-family: Cambria, serif;")
txtstream.WriteLine("    FONT-SIZE: 12px;")
txtstream.WriteLine("    text-align: left;")
txtstream.WriteLine("    white-Space: nowrap;")
txtstream.WriteLine("}")
txtstream.WriteLine(".th")
txtstream.WriteLine("{")
txtstream.WriteLine("    BORDER-RIGHT: #999999 2px solid;")
txtstream.WriteLine("    PADDING-RIGHT: 6px;")
txtstream.WriteLine("    PADDING-LEFT: 6px;")
txtstream.WriteLine("    FONT-WEIGHT: Bold;")
txtstream.WriteLine("    PADDING-BOTTOM: 6px;")
txtstream.WriteLine("    COLOR: black;")
txtstream.WriteLine("    PADDING-TOP: 6px;")
txtstream.WriteLine("    BORDER-BOTTOM: #999 2px solid;")
txtstream.WriteLine("    BACKGROUND-COLOR: #eeeeee;")
txtstream.WriteLine("    FONT-FAMILY: font-family: Cambria, serif;")
txtstream.WriteLine("    FONT-SIZE: 10px;")
txtstream.WriteLine("    text-align: right;")
txtstream.WriteLine("    white-Space: nowrap;")
txtstream.WriteLine("}")
txtstream.WriteLine("td")
txtstream.WriteLine("{")
txtstream.WriteLine("    BORDER-RIGHT: #999999 3px solid;")
txtstream.WriteLine("    PADDING-RIGHT: 6px;")
txtstream.WriteLine("    PADDING-LEFT: 6px;")
txtstream.WriteLine("    FONT-WEIGHT: Normal;")
txtstream.WriteLine("    PADDING-BOTTOM: 6px;")
txtstream.WriteLine("    COLOR: navy;")
txtstream.WriteLine("    LINE-HEIGHT: 14px;")
txtstream.WriteLine("    PADDING-TOP: 6px;")
txtstream.WriteLine("    BORDER-BOTTOM: #999 1px solid;")
txtstream.WriteLine("    BACKGROUND-COLOR: #eeeeee;")
txtstream.WriteLine("    FONT-FAMILY: font-family: Cambria, serif;")
txtstream.WriteLine("    FONT-SIZE: 12px;")
txtstream.WriteLine("    text-align: left;")
txtstream.WriteLine("    white-Space: nowrap;")
txtstream.WriteLine("}")
```

```
txtstream.WriteLine("div")
txtstream.WriteLine("{")
txtstream.WriteLine("   BORDER-RIGHT: #999999 3px solid;")
txtstream.WriteLine("   PADDING-RIGHT: 6px;")
txtstream.WriteLine("   PADDING-LEFT: 6px;")
txtstream.WriteLine("   FONT-WEIGHT: Normal;")
txtstream.WriteLine("   PADDING-BOTTOM: 6px;")
txtstream.WriteLine("   COLOR: white;")
txtstream.WriteLine("   PADDING-TOP: 6px;")
txtstream.WriteLine("   BORDER-BOTTOM: #999 1px solid;")
txtstream.WriteLine("   BACKGROUND-COLOR: navy;")
txtstream.WriteLine("   FONT-FAMILY: font-family: Cambria, serif;")
txtstream.WriteLine("   FONT-SIZE: 10px;")
txtstream.WriteLine("   text-align: left;")
txtstream.WriteLine("   white-Space: nowrap;")
txtstream.WriteLine("}")
txtstream.WriteLine("span")
txtstream.WriteLine("{")
txtstream.WriteLine("   BORDER-RIGHT: #999999 3px solid;")
txtstream.WriteLine("   PADDING-RIGHT: 3px;")
txtstream.WriteLine("   PADDING-LEFT: 3px;")
txtstream.WriteLine("   FONT-WEIGHT: Normal;")
txtstream.WriteLine("   PADDING-BOTTOM: 3px;")
txtstream.WriteLine("   COLOR: white;")
txtstream.WriteLine("   PADDING-TOP: 3px;")
txtstream.WriteLine("   BORDER-BOTTOM: #999 1px solid;")
txtstream.WriteLine("   BACKGROUND-COLOR: navy;")
txtstream.WriteLine("   FONT-FAMILY: font-family: Cambria, serif;")
txtstream.WriteLine("   FONT-SIZE: 10px;")
txtstream.WriteLine("   text-align: left;")
txtstream.WriteLine("   white-Space: nowrap;")
txtstream.WriteLine("   display:inline-block;")
txtstream.WriteLine("   width: 100%;")
txtstream.WriteLine("}")
txtstream.WriteLine("textarea")
txtstream.WriteLine("{")
txtstream.WriteLine("   BORDER-RIGHT: #999999 3px solid;")
txtstream.WriteLine("   PADDING-RIGHT: 3px;")
txtstream.WriteLine("   PADDING-LEFT: 3px;")
txtstream.WriteLine("   FONT-WEIGHT: Normal;")
```

```
txtstream.WriteLine("    PADDING-BOTTOM: 3px;")
txtstream.WriteLine("    COLOR: white;")
txtstream.WriteLine("    PADDING-TOP: 3px;")
txtstream.WriteLine("    BORDER-BOTTOM: #999 1px solid;")
txtstream.WriteLine("    BACKGROUND-COLOR: navy;")
txtstream.WriteLine("    FONT-FAMILY: font-family: Cambria, serif;")
txtstream.WriteLine("    FONT-SIZE: 10px;")
txtstream.WriteLine("    text-align: left;")
txtstream.WriteLine("    white-Space: nowrap;")
txtstream.WriteLine("    width: 100%;")
txtstream.WriteLine("}")
txtstream.WriteLine("select")
txtstream.WriteLine("{")
txtstream.WriteLine("    BORDER-RIGHT: #999999 3px solid;")
txtstream.WriteLine("    PADDING-RIGHT: 6px;")
txtstream.WriteLine("    PADDING-LEFT: 6px;")
txtstream.WriteLine("    FONT-WEIGHT: Normal;")
txtstream.WriteLine("    PADDING-BOTTOM: 6px;")
txtstream.WriteLine("    COLOR: white;")
txtstream.WriteLine("    PADDING-TOP: 6px;")
txtstream.WriteLine("    BORDER-BOTTOM: #999 1px solid;")
txtstream.WriteLine("    BACKGROUND-COLOR: navy;")
txtstream.WriteLine("    FONT-FAMILY: font-family: Cambria, serif;")
txtstream.WriteLine("    FONT-SIZE: 10px;")
txtstream.WriteLine("    text-align: left;")
txtstream.WriteLine("    white-Space: nowrap;")
txtstream.WriteLine("    width: 100%;")
txtstream.WriteLine("}")
txtstream.WriteLine("input")
txtstream.WriteLine("{")
txtstream.WriteLine("    BORDER-RIGHT: #999999 3px solid;")
txtstream.WriteLine("    PADDING-RIGHT: 3px;")
txtstream.WriteLine("    PADDING-LEFT: 3px;")
txtstream.WriteLine("    FONT-WEIGHT: Bold;")
txtstream.WriteLine("    PADDING-BOTTOM: 3px;")
txtstream.WriteLine("    COLOR: white;")
txtstream.WriteLine("    PADDING-TOP: 3px;")
txtstream.WriteLine("    BORDER-BOTTOM: #999 1px solid;")
txtstream.WriteLine("    BACKGROUND-COLOR: navy;")
txtstream.WriteLine("    FONT-FAMILY: font-family: Cambria, serif;")
```

```
txtstream.WriteLine("    FONT-SIZE: 12px;")
txtstream.WriteLine("    text-align: left;")
txtstream.WriteLine("    display:table-cell;")
txtstream.WriteLine("    white-Space: nowrap;")
txtstream.WriteLine("    width: 100%;")
txtstream.WriteLine("}")
txtstream.WriteLine("h1 {")
txtstream.WriteLine("color: antiquewhite;")
txtstream.WriteLine("text-shadow: 1px 1px 1px black;")
txtstream.WriteLine("padding: 3px;")
txtstream.WriteLine("text-align: center;")
txtstream.WriteLine("box-shadow: in2px 2px 5px rgba(0,0,0,0.5), in-
2px -2px 5px rgba(255,255,255,0.5);")
txtstream.WriteLine("}")
txtstream.WriteLine("</style>")

    Case "ShadowBox"

txtstream.WriteLine("<style type='text/css'>")
txtstream.WriteLine("body")
txtstream.WriteLine("{")
txtstream.WriteLine("    PADDING-RIGHT: 0px;")
txtstream.WriteLine("    PADDING-LEFT: 0px;")
txtstream.WriteLine("    PADDING-BOTTOM: 0px;")
txtstream.WriteLine("    MARGIN: 0px;")
txtstream.WriteLine("    COLOR: #333;")
txtstream.WriteLine("    PADDING-TOP: 0px;")
txtstream.WriteLine("    FONT-FAMILY: verdana, arial, helvetica, sans-
serif;")
txtstream.WriteLine("}")
txtstream.WriteLine("table")
txtstream.WriteLine("{")
txtstream.WriteLine("    BORDER-RIGHT: #999999 1px solid;")
txtstream.WriteLine("    PADDING-RIGHT: 1px;")
txtstream.WriteLine("    PADDING-LEFT: 1px;")
txtstream.WriteLine("    PADDING-BOTTOM: 1px;")
txtstream.WriteLine("    LINE-HEIGHT: 8px;")
txtstream.WriteLine("    PADDING-TOP: 1px;")
txtstream.WriteLine("    BORDER-BOTTOM: #999 1px solid;")
txtstream.WriteLine("    BACKGROUND-COLOR: #eeeeee;")
```

```
        txtstream.WriteLine("
filter:progid:DXImageTransform.Microsoft.Shadow(color='silver',        Direction=135,
Strength=16)")
        txtstream.WriteLine("}")
        txtstream.WriteLine("th")
        txtstream.WriteLine("{")
        txtstream.WriteLine("   BORDER-RIGHT: #999999 3px solid;")
        txtstream.WriteLine("   PADDING-RIGHT: 6px;")
        txtstream.WriteLine("   PADDING-LEFT: 6px;")
        txtstream.WriteLine("   FONT-WEIGHT: Bold;")
        txtstream.WriteLine("   FONT-SIZE: 14px;")
        txtstream.WriteLine("   PADDING-BOTTOM: 6px;")
        txtstream.WriteLine("   COLOR: darkred;")
        txtstream.WriteLine("   LINE-HEIGHT: 14px;")
        txtstream.WriteLine("   PADDING-TOP: 6px;")
        txtstream.WriteLine("   BORDER-BOTTOM: #999 1px solid;")
        txtstream.WriteLine("   BACKGROUND-COLOR: #eeeeee;")
        txtstream.WriteLine("   FONT-FAMILY: font-family: Cambria, serif;")
        txtstream.WriteLine("   FONT-SIZE: 12px;")
        txtstream.WriteLine("   text-align: left;")
        txtstream.WriteLine("   white-Space: nowrap;")
        txtstream.WriteLine("}")
        txtstream.WriteLine(".th")
        txtstream.WriteLine("{")
        txtstream.WriteLine("   BORDER-RIGHT: #999999 2px solid;")
        txtstream.WriteLine("   PADDING-RIGHT: 6px;")
        txtstream.WriteLine("   PADDING-LEFT: 6px;")
        txtstream.WriteLine("   FONT-WEIGHT: Bold;")
        txtstream.WriteLine("   PADDING-BOTTOM: 6px;")
        txtstream.WriteLine("   COLOR: black;")
        txtstream.WriteLine("   PADDING-TOP: 6px;")
        txtstream.WriteLine("   BORDER-BOTTOM: #999 2px solid;")
        txtstream.WriteLine("   BACKGROUND-COLOR: #eeeeee;")
        txtstream.WriteLine("   FONT-FAMILY: font-family: Cambria, serif;")
        txtstream.WriteLine("   FONT-SIZE: 10px;")
        txtstream.WriteLine("   text-align: right;")
        txtstream.WriteLine("   white-Space: nowrap;")
        txtstream.WriteLine("}")
        txtstream.WriteLine("td")
        txtstream.WriteLine("{")
```

```
txtstream.WriteLine("   BORDER-RIGHT: #999999 3px solid;")
txtstream.WriteLine("   PADDING-RIGHT: 6px;")
txtstream.WriteLine("   PADDING-LEFT: 6px;")
txtstream.WriteLine("   FONT-WEIGHT: Normal;")
txtstream.WriteLine("   PADDING-BOTTOM: 6px;")
txtstream.WriteLine("   COLOR: navy;")
txtstream.WriteLine("   LINE-HEIGHT: 14px;")
txtstream.WriteLine("   PADDING-TOP: 6px;")
txtstream.WriteLine("   BORDER-BOTTOM: #999 1px solid;")
txtstream.WriteLine("   BACKGROUND-COLOR: #eeeeee;")
txtstream.WriteLine("   FONT-FAMILY: font-family: Cambria, serif;")
txtstream.WriteLine("   FONT-SIZE: 12px;")
txtstream.WriteLine("   text-align: left;")
txtstream.WriteLine("   white-Space: nowrap;")
txtstream.WriteLine("}")
txtstream.WriteLine("div")
txtstream.WriteLine("{")
txtstream.WriteLine("   BORDER-RIGHT: #999999 3px solid;")
txtstream.WriteLine("   PADDING-RIGHT: 6px;")
txtstream.WriteLine("   PADDING-LEFT: 6px;")
txtstream.WriteLine("   FONT-WEIGHT: Normal;")
txtstream.WriteLine("   PADDING-BOTTOM: 6px;")
txtstream.WriteLine("   COLOR: white;")
txtstream.WriteLine("   PADDING-TOP: 6px;")
txtstream.WriteLine("   BORDER-BOTTOM: #999 1px solid;")
txtstream.WriteLine("   BACKGROUND-COLOR: navy;")
txtstream.WriteLine("   FONT-FAMILY: font-family: Cambria, serif;")
txtstream.WriteLine("   FONT-SIZE: 10px;")
txtstream.WriteLine("   text-align: left;")
txtstream.WriteLine("   white-Space: nowrap;")
txtstream.WriteLine("}")
txtstream.WriteLine("span")
txtstream.WriteLine("{")
txtstream.WriteLine("   BORDER-RIGHT: #999999 3px solid;")
txtstream.WriteLine("   PADDING-RIGHT: 3px;")
txtstream.WriteLine("   PADDING-LEFT: 3px;")
txtstream.WriteLine("   FONT-WEIGHT: Normal;")
txtstream.WriteLine("   PADDING-BOTTOM: 3px;")
txtstream.WriteLine("   COLOR: white;")
txtstream.WriteLine("   PADDING-TOP: 3px;")
```

```
txtstream.WriteLine("    BORDER-BOTTOM: #999 1px solid;")
txtstream.WriteLine("    BACKGROUND-COLOR: navy;")
txtstream.WriteLine("    FONT-FAMILY: font-family: Cambria, serif;")
txtstream.WriteLine("    FONT-SIZE: 10px;")
txtstream.WriteLine("    text-align: left;")
txtstream.WriteLine("    white-Space: nowrap;")
txtstream.WriteLine("    display: inline-block;")
txtstream.WriteLine("    width: 100%;")
txtstream.WriteLine("}")
txtstream.WriteLine("textarea")
txtstream.WriteLine("{")
txtstream.WriteLine("    BORDER-RIGHT: #999999 3px solid;")
txtstream.WriteLine("    PADDING-RIGHT: 3px;")
txtstream.WriteLine("    PADDING-LEFT: 3px;")
txtstream.WriteLine("    FONT-WEIGHT: Normal;")
txtstream.WriteLine("    PADDING-BOTTOM: 3px;")
txtstream.WriteLine("    COLOR: white;")
txtstream.WriteLine("    PADDING-TOP: 3px;")
txtstream.WriteLine("    BORDER-BOTTOM: #999 1px solid;")
txtstream.WriteLine("    BACKGROUND-COLOR: navy;")
txtstream.WriteLine("    FONT-FAMILY: font-family: Cambria, serif;")
txtstream.WriteLine("    FONT-SIZE: 10px;")
txtstream.WriteLine("    text-align: left;")
txtstream.WriteLine("    white-Space: nowrap;")
txtstream.WriteLine("    width: 100%;")
txtstream.WriteLine("}")
txtstream.WriteLine("select")
txtstream.WriteLine("{")
txtstream.WriteLine("    BORDER-RIGHT: #999999 3px solid;")
txtstream.WriteLine("    PADDING-RIGHT: 6px;")
txtstream.WriteLine("    PADDING-LEFT: 6px;")
txtstream.WriteLine("    FONT-WEIGHT: Normal;")
txtstream.WriteLine("    PADDING-BOTTOM: 6px;")
txtstream.WriteLine("    COLOR: white;")
txtstream.WriteLine("    PADDING-TOP: 6px;")
txtstream.WriteLine("    BORDER-BOTTOM: #999 1px solid;")
txtstream.WriteLine("    BACKGROUND-COLOR: navy;")
txtstream.WriteLine("    FONT-FAMILY: font-family: Cambria, serif;")
txtstream.WriteLine("    FONT-SIZE: 10px;")
txtstream.WriteLine("    text-align: left;")
```

```
txtstream.WriteLine("    white-Space: nowrap;")
txtstream.WriteLine("    width: 100%;")
txtstream.WriteLine("}")
txtstream.WriteLine("input")
txtstream.WriteLine("{")
txtstream.WriteLine("    BORDER-RIGHT: #999999 3px solid;")
txtstream.WriteLine("    PADDING-RIGHT: 3px;")
txtstream.WriteLine("    PADDING-LEFT: 3px;")
txtstream.WriteLine("    FONT-WEIGHT: Bold;")
txtstream.WriteLine("    PADDING-BOTTOM: 3px;")
txtstream.WriteLine("    COLOR: white;")
txtstream.WriteLine("    PADDING-TOP: 3px;")
txtstream.WriteLine("    BORDER-BOTTOM: #999 1px solid;")
txtstream.WriteLine("    BACKGROUND-COLOR: navy;")
txtstream.WriteLine("    FONT-FAMILY: font-family: Cambria, serif;")
txtstream.WriteLine("    FONT-SIZE: 12px;")
txtstream.WriteLine("    text-align: left;")
txtstream.WriteLine("    display: table-cell;")
txtstream.WriteLine("    white-Space: nowrap;")
txtstream.WriteLine("    width: 100%;")
txtstream.WriteLine("}")
txtstream.WriteLine("h1 {")
txtstream.WriteLine("color: antiquewhite;")
txtstream.WriteLine("text-shadow: 1px 1px 1px black;")
txtstream.WriteLine("padding: 3px;")
txtstream.WriteLine("text-align: center;")
txtstream.WriteLine("box-shadow: in2px 2px 5px rgba(0,0,0,0.5), in-
2px -2px 5px rgba(255,255,255,0.5);")
txtstream.WriteLine("}")
txtstream.WriteLine("</style>")

Case "Customized"

txtstream.WriteLine("<style type='text/css'>")
txtstream.WriteLine("body")
txtstream.WriteLine("{")
txtstream.WriteLine("    PADDING-RIGHT: 0px;")
txtstream.WriteLine("    PADDING-LEFT: 0px;")
txtstream.WriteLine("    PADDING-BOTTOM: 0px;")
txtstream.WriteLine("    MARGIN: 0px;")
```

```
            txtstream.WriteLine("    COLOR: #333;")
            txtstream.WriteLine("    PADDING-TOP: 0px;")
            txtstream.WriteLine("    FONT-FAMILY: verdana, arial, helvetica, sans-
serif;")
            txtstream.WriteLine("}")
            txtstream.WriteLine("Table")
            txtstream.WriteLine("{")
            txtstream.WriteLine("    BORDER-RIGHT: #999999 1px solid;")
            txtstream.WriteLine("    PADDING-RIGHT: 1px;")
            txtstream.WriteLine("    PADDING-LEFT: 1px;")
            txtstream.WriteLine("    PADDING-BOTTOM: 1px;")
            txtstream.WriteLine("    LINE-HEIGHT: 8px;")
            txtstream.WriteLine("    PADDING-TOP: 1px;")
            txtstream.WriteLine("    BORDER-BOTTOM: #999 1px solid;")
            txtstream.WriteLine("    BACKGROUND-COLOR: #eeeeee;")
            txtstream.WriteLine("
filter:progid:DXImageTransform.Microsoft.Shadow(color='silver',    Direction=135,
Strength=16)")
            txtstream.WriteLine("}")
            txtstream.WriteLine("th")
            txtstream.WriteLine("{")
            txtstream.WriteLine("    BORDER-RIGHT: #999999 3px solid;")
            txtstream.WriteLine("    PADDING-RIGHT: 6px;")
            txtstream.WriteLine("    PADDING-LEFT: 6px;")
            txtstream.WriteLine("    FONT-WEIGHT: Bold;")
            txtstream.WriteLine("    FONT-SIZE: 14px;")
            txtstream.WriteLine("    PADDING-BOTTOM: 6px;")
            txtstream.WriteLine("    COLOR: darkred;")
            txtstream.WriteLine("    LINE-HEIGHT: 14px;")
            txtstream.WriteLine("    PADDING-TOP: 6px;")
            txtstream.WriteLine("    BORDER-BOTTOM: #999 1px solid;")
            txtstream.WriteLine("    BACKGROUND-COLOR: #eeeeee;")
            txtstream.WriteLine("    FONT-FAMILY: font-family: Cambria, serif;")
            txtstream.WriteLine("    FONT-SIZE: 12px;")
            txtstream.WriteLine("    text-align: left;")
            txtstream.WriteLine("    white-Space: nowrap;")
            txtstream.WriteLine("}")
            txtstream.WriteLine(".th")
            txtstream.WriteLine("{")
            txtstream.WriteLine("    BORDER-RIGHT: #999999 2px solid;")
```

```
txtstream.WriteLine("    PADDING-RIGHT: 6px;")
txtstream.WriteLine("    PADDING-LEFT: 6px;")
txtstream.WriteLine("    FONT-WEIGHT: Bold;")
txtstream.WriteLine("    PADDING-BOTTOM: 6px;")
txtstream.WriteLine("    COLOR: black;")
txtstream.WriteLine("    PADDING-TOP: 6px;")
txtstream.WriteLine("    BORDER-BOTTOM: #999 2px solid;")
txtstream.WriteLine("    BACKGROUND-COLOR: #eeeeee;")
txtstream.WriteLine("    FONT-FAMILY: font-family: Cambria, serif;")
txtstream.WriteLine("    FONT-SIZE: 10px;")
txtstream.WriteLine("    text-align: right;")
txtstream.WriteLine("    white-Space: nowrap;")
txtstream.WriteLine("}")
txtstream.WriteLine("td")
txtstream.WriteLine("{")
txtstream.WriteLine("    BORDER-RIGHT: #999999 3px solid;")
txtstream.WriteLine("    PADDING-RIGHT: 6px;")
txtstream.WriteLine("    PADDING-LEFT: 6px;")
txtstream.WriteLine("    FONT-WEIGHT: Normal;")
txtstream.WriteLine("    PADDING-BOTTOM: 6px;")
txtstream.WriteLine("    COLOR: navy;")
txtstream.WriteLine("    LINE-HEIGHT: 14px;")
txtstream.WriteLine("    PADDING-TOP: 6px;")
txtstream.WriteLine("    BORDER-BOTTOM: #999 1px solid;")
txtstream.WriteLine("    BACKGROUND-COLOR: #eeeeee;")
txtstream.WriteLine("    FONT-FAMILY: font-family: Cambria, serif;")
txtstream.WriteLine("    FONT-SIZE: 12px;")
txtstream.WriteLine("    text-align: left;")
txtstream.WriteLine("    white-Space: nowrap;")
txtstream.WriteLine("}")
txtstream.WriteLine("div")
txtstream.WriteLine("{")
txtstream.WriteLine("    BORDER-RIGHT: #999999 3px solid;")
txtstream.WriteLine("    PADDING-RIGHT: 6px;")
txtstream.WriteLine("    PADDING-LEFT: 6px;")
txtstream.WriteLine("    FONT-WEIGHT: Normal;")
txtstream.WriteLine("    PADDING-BOTTOM: 6px;")
txtstream.WriteLine("    COLOR: white;")
txtstream.WriteLine("    PADDING-TOP: 6px;")
txtstream.WriteLine("    BORDER-BOTTOM: #999 1px solid;")
```

```
txtstream.WriteLine("    BACKGROUND-COLOR: navy;")
txtstream.WriteLine("    FONT-FAMILY: font-family: Cambria, serif;")
txtstream.WriteLine("    FONT-SIZE: 10px;")
txtstream.WriteLine("    text-align: left;")
txtstream.WriteLine("    white-Space: nowrap;")
txtstream.WriteLine("}")
txtstream.WriteLine("span")
txtstream.WriteLine("{")
txtstream.WriteLine("    BORDER-RIGHT: #999999 3px solid;")
txtstream.WriteLine("    PADDING-RIGHT: 3px;")
txtstream.WriteLine("    PADDING-LEFT: 3px;")
txtstream.WriteLine("    FONT-WEIGHT: Normal;")
txtstream.WriteLine("    PADDING-BOTTOM: 3px;")
txtstream.WriteLine("    COLOR: white;")
txtstream.WriteLine("    PADDING-TOP: 3px;")
txtstream.WriteLine("    BORDER-BOTTOM: #999 1px solid;")
txtstream.WriteLine("    BACKGROUND-COLOR: navy;")
txtstream.WriteLine("    FONT-FAMILY: font-family: Cambria, serif;")
txtstream.WriteLine("    FONT-SIZE: 10px;")
txtstream.WriteLine("    text-align: left;")
txtstream.WriteLine("    white-Space: nowrap;")
txtstream.WriteLine("    display: inline-block;")
txtstream.WriteLine("    width: 100%;")
txtstream.WriteLine("}")
txtstream.WriteLine("textarea")
txtstream.WriteLine("{")
txtstream.WriteLine("    BORDER-RIGHT: #999999 3px solid;")
txtstream.WriteLine("    PADDING-RIGHT: 3px;")
txtstream.WriteLine("    PADDING-LEFT: 3px;")
txtstream.WriteLine("    FONT-WEIGHT: Normal;")
txtstream.WriteLine("    PADDING-BOTTOM: 3px;")
txtstream.WriteLine("    COLOR: white;")
txtstream.WriteLine("    PADDING-TOP: 3px;")
txtstream.WriteLine("    BORDER-BOTTOM: #999 1px solid;")
txtstream.WriteLine("    BACKGROUND-COLOR: navy;")
txtstream.WriteLine("    FONT-FAMILY: font-family: Cambria, serif;")
txtstream.WriteLine("    FONT-SIZE: 12px;")
txtstream.WriteLine("    text-align: left;")
txtstream.WriteLine("    width: 100%;")
txtstream.WriteLine("}")
```

```
txtstream.WriteLine("select")
txtstream.WriteLine("{")
txtstream.WriteLine("    BORDER-RIGHT: #999999 1px solid;")
txtstream.WriteLine("    PADDING-RIGHT: 1px;")
txtstream.WriteLine("    PADDING-LEFT: 1px;")
txtstream.WriteLine("    FONT-WEIGHT: Normal;")
txtstream.WriteLine("    PADDING-BOTTOM: 1px;")
txtstream.WriteLine("    COLOR: white;")
txtstream.WriteLine("    PADDING-TOP: 1px;")
txtstream.WriteLine("    BORDER-BOTTOM: #999 1px solid;")
txtstream.WriteLine("    BACKGROUND-COLOR: navy;")
txtstream.WriteLine("    FONT-FAMILY: Cambria, serif;")
txtstream.WriteLine("    FONT-SIZE: 12px;")
txtstream.WriteLine("    text-align: left;")
txtstream.WriteLine("    white-Space: nowrap;")
txtstream.WriteLine("    width: 450px;")
txtstream.WriteLine("}")
txtstream.WriteLine("select1")
txtstream.WriteLine("{")
txtstream.WriteLine("    BORDER-RIGHT: #999999 1px solid;")
txtstream.WriteLine("    PADDING-RIGHT: 1px;")
txtstream.WriteLine("    PADDING-LEFT: 1px;")
txtstream.WriteLine("    FONT-WEIGHT: Normal;")
txtstream.WriteLine("    PADDING-BOTTOM: 1px;")
txtstream.WriteLine("    COLOR: white;")
txtstream.WriteLine("    PADDING-TOP: 1px;")
txtstream.WriteLine("    BORDER-BOTTOM: #999 1px solid;")
txtstream.WriteLine("    BACKGROUND-COLOR: navy;")
txtstream.WriteLine("    FONT-FAMILY: Cambria, serif;")
txtstream.WriteLine("    FONT-SIZE: 12px;")
txtstream.WriteLine("    text-align: left;")
txtstream.WriteLine("    white-Space: nowrap;")
txtstream.WriteLine("    width: 450px;")
txtstream.WriteLine("}")
txtstream.WriteLine("select2")
txtstream.WriteLine("{")
txtstream.WriteLine("    BORDER-RIGHT: #999999 1px solid;")
txtstream.WriteLine("    PADDING-RIGHT: 1px;")
txtstream.WriteLine("    PADDING-LEFT: 1px;")
txtstream.WriteLine("    FONT-WEIGHT: Normal;")
```

```
txtstream.WriteLine("    PADDING-BOTTOM: 1px;")
txtstream.WriteLine("    COLOR: white;")
txtstream.WriteLine("    PADDING-TOP: 1px;")
txtstream.WriteLine("    BORDER-BOTTOM: #999 1px solid;")
txtstream.WriteLine("    BACKGROUND-COLOR: navy;")
txtstream.WriteLine("    FONT-FAMILY: Cambria, serif;")
txtstream.WriteLine("    FONT-SIZE: 12px;")
txtstream.WriteLine("    text-align: left;")
txtstream.WriteLine("    white-Space: nowrap;")
txtstream.WriteLine("    width: 450px;")
txtstream.WriteLine("}")
txtstream.WriteLine("select3")
txtstream.WriteLine("{")
txtstream.WriteLine("    BORDER-RIGHT: #999999 1px solid;")
txtstream.WriteLine("    PADDING-RIGHT: 1px;")
txtstream.WriteLine("    PADDING-LEFT: 1px;")
txtstream.WriteLine("    FONT-WEIGHT: Normal;")
txtstream.WriteLine("    PADDING-BOTTOM: 1px;")
txtstream.WriteLine("    COLOR: white;")
txtstream.WriteLine("    PADDING-TOP: 1px;")
txtstream.WriteLine("    BORDER-BOTTOM: #999 1px solid;")
txtstream.WriteLine("    BACKGROUND-COLOR: navy;")
txtstream.WriteLine("    FONT-FAMILY: Cambria, serif;")
txtstream.WriteLine("    FONT-SIZE: 12px;")
txtstream.WriteLine("    text-align: left;")
txtstream.WriteLine("    white-Space: nowrap;")
txtstream.WriteLine("    width: 100px;")
txtstream.WriteLine("}")
txtstream.WriteLine("select4")
txtstream.WriteLine("{")
txtstream.WriteLine("    BORDER-RIGHT: #999999 1px solid;")
txtstream.WriteLine("    PADDING-RIGHT: 1px;")
txtstream.WriteLine("    PADDING-LEFT: 1px;")
txtstream.WriteLine("    FONT-WEIGHT: Normal;")
txtstream.WriteLine("    PADDING-BOTTOM: 1px;")
txtstream.WriteLine("    COLOR: white;")
txtstream.WriteLine("    PADDING-TOP: 1px;")
txtstream.WriteLine("    BORDER-BOTTOM: #999 1px solid;")
txtstream.WriteLine("    BACKGROUND-COLOR: navy;")
txtstream.WriteLine("    FONT-FAMILY: Cambria, serif;")
```

```
txtstream.WriteLine("   FONT-SIZE: 12px;")
txtstream.WriteLine("   text-align: left;")
txtstream.WriteLine("   white-Space: nowrap;")
txtstream.WriteLine("   width: 254px;")
txtstream.WriteLine("}")
txtstream.WriteLine("input")
txtstream.WriteLine("{")
txtstream.WriteLine("   BORDER-RIGHT: #999999 3px solid;")
txtstream.WriteLine("   PADDING-RIGHT: 3px;")
txtstream.WriteLine("   PADDING-LEFT: 3px;")
txtstream.WriteLine("   FONT-WEIGHT: Bold;")
txtstream.WriteLine("   PADDING-BOTTOM: 3px;")
txtstream.WriteLine("   COLOR: white;")
txtstream.WriteLine("   PADDING-TOP: 3px;")
txtstream.WriteLine("   BORDER-BOTTOM: #999 1px solid;")
txtstream.WriteLine("   BACKGROUND-COLOR: navy;")
txtstream.WriteLine("   FONT-FAMILY: font-family: Cambria, serif;")
txtstream.WriteLine("   FONT-SIZE: 12px;")
txtstream.WriteLine("   text-align: left;")
txtstream.WriteLine("   display: table-cell;")
txtstream.WriteLine("   white-Space: nowrap;")
txtstream.WriteLine("   width: 100%;")
txtstream.WriteLine("}")
txtstream.WriteLine("</style>")

        End Select

End Sub

</script>

</body>
</html>
```

Above this line is where it ends.

Merry Christmas!